Laughter With

For My Family

*I hope you laugh I hope you cry
I hope you never ask me why.*

*The answer is clear no need to fear,
you are the ones that I hold dear.*

*Come read with me and you will see,
the way that it will always be.*

*You're in my heart you're in my head,
you'll see it all when you have read.*

*What times we had not all were bad,
I hope it doesn't leave you sad.*

*We were a team a mighty crew,
these memories I write for you.*

1. THE END

He's dead.

After all the years of waiting, and yes I have to say, sometimes wishing, he's actually dead. A death that was no less traumatic for having been expected for the last forty years.

We'd talked about his death often, it was one of his favourite subjects. "Just lay me out on the snooker table at the club and have a drink on me," He'd say. So we thought we were prepared, but he didn't die the way any of us expected.

I'm talking about my dad. He's been dying ever since I can remember, so I grew up with the expectation that he wouldn't always be around.

Every Christmas he would say, "You'd better make the most of it because I won't be here next year." Make the most of what, I often wondered? I never thought for a moment we couldn't manage without him, he contributed little to our family life.

He always said he would die a young man, but there he was almost eighty-two years old. I don't know whether he was disappointed or pleased at having lived so long. He certainly didn't look after himself, he smoked and drank heavily most of his life. He had his first heart attack when he was only thirty-nine.

I was five years old and I remember him being taken away in the ambulance. He'd refused to get on the stretcher, said he didn't want to make a show of himself in front of all the neighbours who'd all come out to see what was going on. He climbed in unaided with a blanket around his shoulders, complaining the whole time. Mum had to run to the shops to buy him some pajamas for the hospital. She didn't think they'd appreciate him wandering around in just his vest like he did at home.

There were countless trips to the hospital over the years so the pajamas got a lot of use. They were kept folded neatly in the drawer until the next time came around. We'd get the call and we'd all come running. The doctors would say, "It's touch and go," or, "It could go either way." So we'd be left to wait, and wonder what life would be like without him. But he always got better, the boy who cried wolf had nothing on him.

On those occasions, while I was waiting for him to decide whether he was going to live or die, my mind would be full of questions. Did I really want him to die? Would I be sad if he did? Were there things I hadn't said to him that I needed to say? Were there things he hadn't said to me, that I needed to hear? This would go round and round in my head. Then we'd get the news that he was going to live, but instead of confronting these issues once he was well, I would put them to the back of my mind, glad I didn't have to deal with them, until next time.

But next time we didn't get the call. Dad died in a rest-home in Australia, he was far from home, with no family around him. I'd always said he would die a lonely old man. I don't think that's what I wanted for him. Or did I? Did I think it was no more than he deserved?

And so after all the drama he put us through over the years, he died peacefully in his own bed. At one time I might have said that was too good for him, but did I really mean that?

Dad and I hadn't spoken for a few months before he died. He blamed me for putting him in the rest-home, and I was angry at being blamed for something that wasn't my fault. I hated the way things had turned out for him, but he'd brought it all on himself. Still, he was my dad, and as Father's day was coming up, I thought it was the ideal time to bury the hatchet, and give him a call.

Sleep didn't come easy for me the night before I was to phone. I lay awake for hours thinking about what I would say, and what he might say to me. Old age had mellowed him, but our history together made me wary. When dad had you in his sights, he showed no mercy, he could say the cruelest things. It was like he could read your mind, find the most vulnerable spot and strike. Whoever said, "Sticks and stones may break your bones but words will never hurt you," didn't know my dad.

A bruise will heal, words stay in your head and haunt you forever, especially when those words are spoken by your Father.

Still, I knew he would be pleased to hear from me on Father's Day. If only I'd known while I was wrestling with my thoughts, he was dying, alone.

The phone rang at one-thirty in the morning. It was my sister Catherine. "Dad's just died," She said.

It was hard for her. She'd been planning to bring him home, back to New Zealand so she could look after him. It was going to be her time with him, time he'd never given her. She was looking forward to all the special times they would have together. She'd found a rest-home close to where she was living so she could call in on her way home from work each day and fuss over him. She'd bought things for his room, and made lots of soup because he was having trouble eating. She was just waiting for clearance from the doctor to say he could go on a plane when she got the call that he'd died.

She was inconsolable. She said, "He can't be dead, I've made soup!"

Laughter With The Tears

Happy Fathers Day

I wanted to say Happy Fathers Day
The silence between us would not go away,
unless I took charge and made the first move,
to pick up the phone, I knew you'd approve

I'd wait till tomorrow, rehearse what to say,
make sure you knew everything was ok.
Words said in anger never meant to be heard,
couldn't diminish the fact that you cared.

I went to sleep with you on my mind,
then at midnight awoke, not surprised to find
You'd come for a visit, you couldn't wait
time had run out, that was your fate.

And when the phone rang, I knew that you'd gone.
I'd missed my last chance, nothing more to be done.
But your presence was felt as you stood by my door,
you'd found a way through to see me once more.

You visited often, no rest for you yet,
tried to make up for the last time we met.
I could feel your anguish, your need to explain,
but no need for that, I'm just glad you came.

2. RETROSPECTIVE

I must admit I felt a bit cheated when dad died. He'd gotten away on me before I had a chance to reproach him for all his wrongdoing over the years. Not that I ever would have I don't suppose, there certainly plenty of opportunity while he was alive. But I was still frightened of him, and even more frightened of hurting him. He had such a knack of making you feel sorry for him. He got away with everything, he was rarely ever brought to task.

And now he'd gotten away with the ultimate, he was resting in peace, while I was left in turmoil. It's hard to live your life never knowing if someone ever loved you. And then they die never having told you.

My sister Rosaleen would always say that I should tell dad I loved him before it was too late. This didn't make any sense to me, when what I really wanted to tell him was that I hated him. I ended up telling him neither one thing, or the other, and was left wondering if I really felt one thing, or the other. I didn't know you could love someone one minute, and hate them the next, I thought it was all or nothing, you had to choose. Nothing is ever black or white, there are many shades of grey in between. It's those shades of grey I'm writing about, and crying about, and grieving over.

You can't love someone who's hurt you unless you are prepared to forgive. But then is there even any point, when the person you can't forgive, doesn't seem to know, or care that they've done anything wrong?

Sometimes we are so closed up and bitter from past experiences we're afraid to let our guard down and give someone a second chance. You do have to protect yourself, but being unforgiving can poison your soul. At some stage in my life I stopped giving my approval and love to my dad, not realising that sometimes you have to give to receive.

A child is born with nothing but love in their heart for their parents, its up to the parents to nurture that love and help it to grow. My love for my dad started to erode early on in my childhood. Even so, I always hoped it would return, I didn't want to lose it. But I realise now that it's impossible to hate your father, because the child inside you wants so much to love him. Young children are optimistic, they are forever hopeful things will get better, and when they do, even if it's only for a few moments, they accept it and are grateful for it however long it lasts. They don't hold a grudge.

Unfortunately, as they get older optimism starts to fade. It gets much harder to hang onto, and eventually it disappears altogether. What any child wants is a Father who loves them and treats them well.

Now that my dad is dead he can't hurt me anymore, and the anger I had towards him died with him, leaving me free to remember him as the father I always wanted him to be, the father I glimpsed when I was a small child.

Love You, Hate You

I could love you one minute, and hate you the next.

Mixed emotions ran through me, and left me so vexed.

A kind word from you, could make me stand tall.

But also leave me with so far to fall.

I'd be first in line when you gave out the praise.

Taking care to hold back, when I saw your hand raise.

How tenuous the love, so fragile the bond.

Never quite knowing how to respond.

3. REMEMBER THE MAN

My dad was a 'product' of his upbringing, a 'product' of his environment, and a 'product' of the times. Maybe there should have been a 'product' recall. I don't want to make excuses for him, but it does explain a lot.

Dad was born on 'Remembrance Day,' and died on 'Father's Day.' Just his way of making sure we couldn't forget him. He was a small man, but very strong with hands of steel, as I was to find out to my detriment over the years. He didn't hit us often, but when he did it was memorable. Mum would tell him, "If there's any smacking to be done around here I'll do it, you don't know your own strength." That was a good rule but he didn't always adhere to it unfortunately for us.

He was an affectionate person, but we didn't get to see much evidence of that as we were always at war with each other. He was very unforgiving, and once he took a dislike to someone that was it, they could never redeem themselves in his eyes.

Dad was born in Trim, County Meath, Ireland in 1926. He never talked much about his childhood except to say how poor he'd been. He told us how he'd had to put boot polish on his feet, and lace up his toes because he didn't have shoes. That was blarney of course, but I'm sure he did go barefoot some of the time, just maybe not in the middle of winter, in the snow.

He told us about the nuns at school with the whips, saying he felt the sting of those more times than he cared to remember.

I did overhear him tell stories about the 'wakes' he went to as a teenager. There would be drinking and singing for three days as people came in to view the deceased and pay their respects. Relatives and friends would take it in turns to watch over the body, someone had to be there at all times in case they were to 'wake' up.

One time dad and a few of his friends were presiding over the body of a hunchback. The man was tied to the bed with a rope hidden under the sheet so he would lay flat. When the three days were up and it didn't look like there was going to be any 'waking' up, the mourners gathered around the bed ready to start the weeping and the wailing. Without anyone seeing, dad took out his penknife and cut the rope. The hunchback lurched forward and sat up, letting out a groan as the air escaped from his body. Everyone ran screaming from the room.

Dad and his friends weren't left in charge of any deceased persons after that.

Even though dad was a Catholic, he wasn't a fanatic, it was just part of who he was, like the black hair on his head. And like the black hair on his head, his religion gradually faded over the years.

Laughter With The Tears

He became disillusioned with his religion as a young man trying to make his way in Ireland in the early years of his marriage. With a pregnant wife about to give birth and a baby in his arms, he walked the streets trying to find a bed for the night. Everyone turned him away when he asked for help, even the Catholic Church. I have heard a similar story, but that one had three wise men and a donkey.

Eventually, a kind lady took pity on them and gave them a room on the top floor of her boarding house. My brother John was born that night, but thankfully not in a stable, because mum haemorrhaged giving birth and could have died if it wasn't for the landlady looking after her. She took care of mum and the two babies for two weeks while dad went out looking for work. There are angels in the world, you don't have to go to church to find them.

So it's not surprising that every Sunday dad would deposit us at the door of the church, and go around the corner to the pub. We would meet him afterward and walk home together, always stopping at the shop for a packet of sweets.

The parish priest would come to our house once a week for a visit, and to collect a donation. We'd see him coming down the street and we'd sound the alarm. Catherine and I would keep him talking on the front doorstep long enough for dad to duck out the back and go to the pub. I don't think they ever met.

The priest might have wondered why we were always in the house alone, but he never said anything.

Dad liked to have money jingling in his pockets, and he was full of blarney. He loved the rain, a prerequisite if you're Irish, and he would rub his hands with glee and jump into bed so he could lie there listening to it spattering on the roof. He also loved the sun, and when we got to New Zealand, would sit outside for hours with his pale Irish skin baking and blistering. One thing he didn't love, was being called 'Paddy.'

Dad never called anyone by their name. It was always, 'The queer one.' It wasn't gender specific, and strangely enough, we always seemed to know who he was talking about. If he didn't like someone, they were called a 'gobshite,' dad knew a lot of those. Then there were the 'Bad bastards,' they were much worse than 'gobshites.' Being a 'Bad bastard' showed some intent, and there was no redemption for them in his eyes.

Living with mum for years in the big city polished off a few of the rough edges. She didn't like swearing and would always tell him off. He did still swear a fair bit, but he only used the 'F' word on special occasions. He didn't say it the Irish way though.

We could never get a simple yes or no answer out of him. When asked if he wanted anything, he would say, "I could do," or "I don't mind."

I've heard it said that at least one person in every Irish family has 'the sight' or 'the third eye,' dad definitely did. We never told him anything, but he knew everything. When we asked him how he knew something he would just say he 'didn't come down in the last shower.' It was uncanny how he knew things, he could size a person up with one glance, it was always negative. He could look at a newborn baby and say, "He'll end up in jail." He was usually right.

Dad could never find anything nice to say about anyone, everyone was a 'halfwit,' 'not right in the head,' or 'not the full quid.' Anyone not attractive enough for his liking 'had a face like a slapped arse,' and anyone successful was 'an imposter.'

The 'halfwits' encompassed half the population. Dad thought all 'halfwits,' and anyone not quite right in the head should get 'the needle.' He was a big fan of euthanasia for any poor unfortunate souls who didn't measure up to his exacting standards. To his credit, he did say if he ever got to the stage where he was incapable, then he would be happy to have 'the needle' himself. I was quick to offer my services, anything to oblige.

Dad hated listening to argy-bargy and women yapping in his ear. "You must have been vaccinated with a gramophone needle," he'd say.

He was always strumming and tapping on the arm of his chair, like he always had a tune in his head. It was probably 'Shinamarinky,' dad sang that to us all the time when we were little. Sometimes if he was in a good mood he would come out with a 'diddley aye diddley aye' and do a little jig with his feet.

Getting dad the perfect gift was a lifelong quest for me and Catherine. When we were small mum would give us money to buy him a Christmas present. We would always buy him a packet of Sun Valley tobacco for his role cigarettes, wrap it up and hang it on the tree.

On Christmas mornings we would wait excitedly for him to wake up so we could give it to him. Dad never opened his present, he said he knew what it was so there was no need. It was so disappointing, we didn't remember we'd given him the same thing every year.

One year we organised a surprise birthday for him. Catherine made a cake. We turned all the lights out and were hiding behind the couch when he came home from work. He came into the living room and put the light on, we all jumped out yelling, "Happy birthday!" "It's tomorrow," he said, sitting down and turning the telly on.

Dad wasn't at peace with the world and he had no patience. Everything seemed to upset him and make him angry. He would work himself up into a lather about things that were nothing to do with him.

In his later years he would stand at the window of his house watching the street complaining that the neighbours were going out too often. "He's going out again! He's only just come in an hour ago, where's he think he's goin now? Gobshite!"

The Irish are inventive when it comes to giving directions, usually resulting in you never finding your destination. Dad didn't have this problem, he was an expert at giving directions. He would guide you by telling you all the pubs you'd pass along the way. There was a pub on every corner, and he knew them all.

Dad was nothing if not consistent. He held the same views about everything, and everyone, all his life. You could talk till you were blue in the face but you could never convince him of anything once he'd made up his mind. And he was full of eternal pessimism.

I had a big discussion with him one day about how the Irish economy was booming. They even have a name for it I told him, 'The Celtic Tiger.' He wouldn't have it. "That just benefits the rich," He said. "The rich get richer and the poor stay poor. Ireland's finished, I wouldn't like to go back there now." I said, "Come on dad, you haven't been there for thirty years, things have changed." I tried to explain the ripple effect. How those rich people needed housekeepers and nannies. They'd want nice restaurants and cafés to eat out in, and taxis to take them home. It all created jobs for the less fortunate.

He seemed to be listening and I thought I'd convinced him until later in the day I overheard him talking to someone. He was saying, "Ireland's finished, I wouldn't like to go back there now." As it turned out, dad was right as usual. The Celtic Tiger collapsed along with the economy.

Dad thought it was good to get diseases. Measles, mumps, rubella, the nastier the better, he said it cleaned out the system.

According to him he'd never eaten a decent meal in his life, it was always muck, cold, or raw. He complained about every meal mum made him, and never tired of telling her his Mammy was a good cook.

The last time he stayed with Catherine, three years before he died, she cooked him his favourite meal. I know she would have put a lot of effort into it to make it just right. He took one look at it and said, "Well I'm dead ungry but I'm not eating that shite."

The only thing dad was ever interested in was where his next drink was coming from, the price of beer, and where his next drink was coming from. He despised men who didn't drink, and he despised women who did.

I think it's fair to say 'The drink' had the starring role in his life. It was a fickle friend, there was always too much, or not enough.

I would hear people say, "It's 'the drink' that does it," or, "I blame 'the drink' myself," or, "It's just 'the drink' talking." It seemed to me 'the drink' had a lot to answer for. It ruined all our Christmases, and it made me afraid of certain times of the day when it was 'chucking out time' at the pub. I'd sit quietly waiting to see if 'the drink' had been kind to dad and put him in a good mood. More often than not he would come home happy enough, but the day would usually end in tears.

I soon grew to hate 'the drink' and the problems it caused, so dad featured less and less in my life as I got older. I decided there wasn't enough room in it for him and 'the drink,' and I knew I could never have one without the other.

Dad was an alcoholic. He would hate me saying that. His definition of an alcoholic was someone who mixed their drinks. His favourite tipple was whiskey, but not the cheap stuff, not that he could afford to be choosey. We could always tell when he'd been drinking whiskey, because funnily enough, he was allergic to it. Mum would say, "You've been at the whiskey again haven't you?" "I have not!" He would say, most indignant. Then he would start to sneeze, and sneeze, and sneeze, giving himself away every time.

Dad was a 'street angel' and a 'house devil.' When he was drunk he was fun, when he was half drunk he was mean, when he was sober he was like a bear with a sore head and was to be avoided at all times.

When he'd had enough to drink he would come home 'Waltzing drunk.' He would sway from one foot to the other, he looked like a dancing bear. That was a bad sign.

I learned early in life how to read the signs and know when to keep out of his way. It's frightening and confusing for a child not knowing what sort of situation they're going to face every day when their drunk father comes home.

Even though he was an alcoholic he wasn't feckless. He went to work every-day regardless of the state of his head. He had a car accident on his way to work one morning because he was still drunk from the night before. He always had a job when there were jobs available, but he didn't always hand over his wages. We lived hand to mouth for many years. Dad would come home on payday and only hand over whatever money was left after the drink. Mum would rush straight out to the shops to buy food.

Dad was a painter and decorator by trade. I loved watching him paint when I was little, cutting in with great precision, his hands were surprisingly steady for an alcoholic, but he was a messy painter. Everything got covered in specks of paint, he never covered anything up. He didn't believe in preparation, that was mum's job.

Laughter With The Tears

There were lots of strikes in England in the seventies, so dad sometimes did   part-time jobs in the evenings to make ends meet. One of the best, or worst jobs he got, depending on how you look at it, was as a bartender in a pub. We would watch him getting ready for work every evening. He looked very swish in his red waistcoat, red dickie bow, and gold armbands, his hair slicked back and shiny with Brylcreem.

He didn't have that job for long. Unfortunately, he didn't remember his prayers, 'Lead us not into temptation, but deliver us from evil.' His employers didn't appreciate the fact that he was 'led into temptation' and was caught drinking on the job. But they were more than happy to 'deliver him from evil,' and sacked him. There was lots of fighting in the house that night when he came home with the bad news.

Dad emigrated three times in his lifetime. From Ireland to England as a young single man, from England to New Zealand when he was forty-six, then to Australia at the ripe old age of seventy-eight. Quite adventurous for someone who never wanted to leave his armchair, or his local pub.

It was never his choice to go, in fact, he definitely didn't want to go to New Zealand. As the time drew near for us to leave he started saying, "Just leave me here with me chair and a bucket." I'm not sure what the bucket was for, he probably thought he wouldn't be able to use the toilet if the power was turned off.

In the seventies we were having power cuts every night. One night mum was at work and dad was on his way out to the pub, leaving us in the dark with just a candle. He said, "Now just remember the power's off so you won't be able to flush the toilet." We believed him.

In the new countries he moved to he just swapped one armchair for another, one local for another, that was as adventurous as he ever got. The politics changed, the beer was different, and he did go from watching soccer to rugby, but otherwise he could have been living anywhere. It made no difference to him as long as he had his drink.

I'd like to say he was an island, but that suggests self-sufficiency, and he was as helpless as a puppy with most things. I'd like to say he was a loner, preferring his own company, but that's not true either, he hated to be left alone. It's just that he loved the drink more, and the drink pushed everyone away, it was a jealous friend.

I found him sitting in the dark one night with a drink in his hand, just him and his best friend I thought. A friend who ostracised him from his family and left him sitting alone in the dark.

I'd been around him for over thirty years but that was the first time I'd noticed he got depressed. The drink would have played a big part in his depression, and also the fact that he was Irish.

They thrive on being maudlin, it's part of their make-up, and I think for the most part they enjoy it. They leave their homeland behind and spend the rest of their lives pining for the 'aul country.' But then who doesn't do that?

Dad was probably sitting there thinking back to the time many years ago in Liverpool, when he had the company of his youngest brother, my Uncle Tommy. He was a funny little man, not much more than five feet tall. Dad came from a family of 'diddy men' and women. Interestingly, before the potato famine, Irish people were one of the tallest people in Europe. They shrank as the diseases of vitamin deficiency like rickets took their toll, they definitely affected dad's family.

Uncle Tommy had missing teeth, missing fingers, and language that could strip paint. He walked around bent forward from the hips with his hands in his pockets, always looking as though he was about to pick something up off the floor. We didn't like Uncle Tommy, he was a bit too free with his hands, but he was also very free with the half-crowns when he'd had a few drinks.

Uncle Tommy came to stay with us a lot. We came downstairs many mornings to find him sleeping, or passed out, on the couch after a big night of drinking. He and dad would get drunk together and sing sad songs. I say sing, it sounded more like dogs howling at the wind.

They'd sing the same song over and over, 'Nobody's Child.' A song about a blind child in an orphanage that no-one will adopt. It never seemed much fun to me, but I suppose even that was better than sitting alone in the dark, knowing most of your family are long dead, and you've alienated your children.

Uncle Tommy, and his sister, Aunty Josie, died young, both only in their fifties. Dad's youngest brother Uncle Sean was only in his forties when he died. Only three out of the six siblings had any children. They were a strange bunch, but quite close in their own way.

I said to dad in his later years, "When people get older they should move closer to their family for support." "My family are all dead," he said.

What was I, 'Scotch mist!'

That summed up the way he made me feel, like we weren't important to him, we were just something that happened to him, something he had no control over. When he was in one of his rages he'd said to me, "I don't know, I've raised four whores." Is that what he thought of his four daughters? Dad should have been proud of his children, then his children could have been proud of themselves.

Laughter With The Tears

He didn't mince his words
níor chuir sé fiacail ann

'Kiss me arse,' he always said.
But why not speak Gaelic, and use instead,
'póg mo thóin,' why didn't he say,
it sounds romantic said that way.

'Just a big gobshite,' or a 'queer one,'
could have translated, 'corr aon.'
No-one would know he was being so rude,
but then what's the point, it could be argued.

He said as he saw it, he didn't care,
his Irish forgotten, no words to compare.
'Droch-chaint' means bad language in his native tongue,
I'm sure he was told that, when he was young.

But as he grew old there was no reprimand,
no-one to stop him, he had a free hand.
To call and denounce everyone he saw fit,
'leath ciall' in Gaelic, in English 'half wit.'

4. MEMORIES

Running away from your past is a little like running away from a house fire, you feel you have to run and save yourself from being swallowed up by the flames, or by the emotional backlash of your memories. You don't want to re-visit those memories, because the embers still smoulder with fear and resentment long after the fire has gone out.

When enough time has passed and you feel strong enough to go back and see the devastation caused, you can finally start to sift through the ashes, or the darkest recesses of your memory. You find little mementos buried there under layers of ash, or layers of pain and rejection. Things from your past you thought were lost forever, and they bring back happy memories. You can finally put the wreckage of the past behind you, and take those mementos with you into the future, to remind you of the good things that weren't destroyed, things that were left behind for you to find when you were ready to start looking.

It's a strange feeling when someone you've known your whole life, dies, it's a bit like being cut adrift. In one sense there is a certain freedom, you don't have to wait and hope for the approval that never comes, the validation that you're okay and that you are loved. But then there is the sadness when you realise it's never going to come now.

When someone is alive, the hurt they caused and the resentment you feel towards them stays alive too, but when they die it just seems to disappear. It's a relief to let it go. You can finally move on without being weighed down by it all. You find yourself thinking mostly about the good times, and it's surprising to find there may have been more than you thought.

So you start to search your memory. Maybe the approval and love did come but you weren't paying attention. Maybe it was in the small things, the simple gestures that don't mean much at the time and are easily overlooked. That's when the soul searching begins. You look back and you try to see things with different eyes, more forgiving and understanding eyes. Or even just through the eyes of the adult you have become. You try to put things in perspective and see them for what they were, or might have been.

I keep remembering things from my childhood and I want to ask dad about them. Were they as they seemed or have I embellished them in my mind over the years?

Would he care to remember giving me my first cigarette when I was five, or buying me my first drink in a pub on my thirteenth birthday? And what about stealing? He didn't exactly teach me to steal, but kids do learn by example. Luckily I didn't become an alcoholic, or turn into a thief, well not for long anyway. And I didn't start smoking until I was ten.

I wonder if he ever remembered the time I took ten years off his life. It was Easter weekend and we'd just come back from church so I was all dressed up in my Sunday best. Mum said I wasn't allowed to go across the road to play with my friend because she didn't want me getting dirty. Aunty Betty was coming for tea so we had to look respectable. Not happy with that outcome, I did what any three-year-old child would do, I went and asked my dad. He said yes I could go, so I quickly ran out of the gate, across the road, and straight into the path of an oncoming car. The car stopped just inches away from me. Dad was standing at the gate and saw the whole thing. He ran over, picked me up and hugged me tight to his chest, then he went and apologised to the driver of the car.

Later in the day, I heard him talking to my Aunty Betty, his sister. He was saying, "God Jesus! She was nearly killed in front of me very eyes. It's taken ten year off me life that has." I'd like to apologise to him for that. If I hadn't taken ten years of his life, he could have lived until he was almost ninety-two.

I want to ask dad if he remembers teaching me how to whistle. I couldn't wait to learn so he would be proud of me. Losing my two front teeth held up my progress for a while, and if he sang that song 'All I want for Christmas is me two front teeth' once, he sang it a hundred times. But still, he was there to listen when I finally did it.

I find it funny he didn't take any interest in me learning to read and write, but whistling, now there's a skill!

I'm sure he would have been impressed with the speed at which I learned to read and write if he'd taken an interest. My very first week of school I tackled the alphabet. I was a natural. It was all going well until we got to the letter Z. The teacher told us it might be a hard letter to remember because it wasn't used in many words. I wondered why they didn't just take it out then if no one used it. The teacher handed out name cards to put on the front of our desks. Imagine my dismay when I saw my name in print for the first time. Suzanne! Not only was it very long, but right in the middle of it was a Z. I looked around at everyone else's name cards, not a Z in sight. It was so unfair, why couldn't I be called Susan like everyone else?

It had been my sister Rosaleen's idea to call me Suzanne. I was number five child, and I think my parents had lost interest by the time I came along. Rosaleen decided on Suzanne because she said it was a bit different, everyone else was called Susan. If only she'd known why, before inflicting it on me, it's easier to spell! Anyway, I decided to use the same tenacity dad taught me when teaching me to whistle. Keep trying, never give up, I was going to conquer that Z, I wasn't going to let it beat me.

Once a year at school we would be given a small brown donation envelope from 'The Little Sisters of the Poor.' If you put twelve pennies in the envelope you could put a cross in all the squares on the back and a black baby in Africa would be named after you.

I was never allowed to put twelve pennies in. With so many brothers and sisters all getting an envelope at the same time it was understandable. So there were no black babies in Africa called Suzanne. I bet they were pleased!

I didn't mind too much not having a black African baby named after me because dad said he was going to adopt one for us to play with. He said it would come in the post. I did wonder how it would fit through the letterbox, but if Father Christmas could fit down the chimney, nothing was impossible. It never turned up of course, just like all the other things he promised us, but we never stopped checking when the postman came.

When I was little I thought dad was great, the best dad anyone could wish for. He was so generous, everything I asked for he said I could have it, nothing was too much trouble. I never got anything of course, but I always believed him and lived in hope.

Dad loved baby talk and made up his own words for things. "You're always getting up to 'mitchery' he'd say, instead of mischief. Or, "Do you want a dink a mink," instead of drink of milk.

On my first morning at school, the teacher asked me if I wanted the free milk or orange juice that was being dished out to all the kids. I didn't dare open my mouth when I heard milk pronounced properly. It wasn't called mink, and I didn't know how to say it, I just had to point. I went home and practiced in the mirror for hours trying to get my tongue around that elusive L.

I don't remember dad ever asking me, how was school, or listening to me read, or admire my new writing skills. Maybe he did and I've just forgotten. You can't remember everything about your childhood, but the things that were important to you do stand out.

So what about the joke!

When I was about seven I thought it was my mission in life to make my dad laugh. Every day I would come home from school with my latest knock-knock joke, or what do you get when you cross one of these with one of those. He never laughed. Finally, I got fed up and said to him, "Why don't you ever laugh at my jokes dad?" He looked at me and said, "I tell you what, if you can make me laugh, I'll give you a pound." I thought WOW! That's such a lot of money, I could buy a whole sweet shop with that.

So off I went and scoured the school playground for jokes. Every day I'd wait excitedly until he got home from work, then I'd stand by the arm of his chair and deliver my latest joke.

He never laughed. Sometimes I'd be laughing so hard I couldn't get the joke out, but even then he didn't laugh. I was like the girl in the fairy tale trying to guess the name of Rumplestiltskin so everything would turn to gold.

After a while I decided I was never going to get that pound so I might as well give up. The next day a boy came up to me in the playground and said he had a new joke for me. The word was out, and everyone was bringing me the latest jokes. I think they all wanted a share in my fortune. I was so disappointed, the boy told me the stupidest joke I'd ever heard, it wasn't a bit funny. I wasn't even going to bother telling it to dad, but that night he said, "So where's me joke today then."

I decided I had nothing to lose so I stood by the arm of his chair and told him the stupid joke. Well, he started to laugh, and he laughed until the tears were rolling down his face. I couldn't believe it. Then he reached into his pocket, took out a pound note and gave it to me. I grabbed it and ran away quickly before he could change his mind. I sat on my bed staring at it, thinking about all the things I could buy with it. It really was a fortune to me. Then I started to feel guilty, I knew we didn't have a lot of money. I went downstairs and found dad in the kitchen, he was still chuckling away. I tried to give the pound note back to him. "No," he said. "You earned it, you keep it."

That pound note was in my possession less than twenty-four hours before my brother John stole it from me, but I didn't care. Whatever I'd bought with it would have lasted five minutes, the memory of that laugh will stay with me for a lifetime.

I know dad would remember letting me drive his brand new Ford Cortina when I was thirteen, because I crashed it through the garage door.

He came home from the pub after an afternoon session. I heard his car pull up in the driveway and I ran out to see if he had any green shield stamps from the garage to stick in the book. Mum was collecting them, you could buy all sorts of interesting things with them.

While I was fossicking in the glove box I jokingly asked dad if I could park the car in the garage. To my amazement, he said yes. I hadn't expected that, I didn't even want to drive the car, but I was so pleased he trusted me that I didn't want to back down, so I jumped into the driver's seat.

The garage had a tilt door and it was shut, so the car needed to be reversed a bit to allow the door to open. Dad put the car into gear and told me to put my left foot on the left pedal, my right foot on the right pedal. He said to release my left foot slowly while pressing harder with my right. I did as I was told, if a bit enthusiastically, and the car shot forward straight through the garage door. Dad had put it into first gear by mistake.

Luckily the car stalled when I took my feet off the pedals. It was a free-standing garage made of concrete slabs and the whole lot could have come down on top of me, I could have been killed. I wouldn't have minded, at least it would have been quick, I thought my life was over anyway.

Dad was so proud of his new car, he'd watched it getting built on the assembly line at Ford Motor Company where he worked. He opened the car door and just told me to get out. I expected to see the rage, those terrifying eyes blazing, but he just looked pale and sick. He was probably imagining the phone call he was going to have to make to mum explaining what had happened. She was away in New Zealand at the time.

Dad blamed himself for letting me drive his car, he never blamed me. He did call me James Bond 007 for the next ten years which I really didn't appreciate, but I suppose it was a small price to pay. He kept the car for fourteen years, so it was a constant reminder to me of that dreadful day.

One day in New Zealand many years later, we were all getting ready to go to Rosaleen's second wedding. Mum didn't see dad's car parked in the driveway and she backed her car out of the garage and ploughed straight into it. The chrome bumper of her Morris Minor embedded itself into the passenger door of dad's beleaguered Cortina.

.

Time stood still. We waited holding our breath, watching the back door expecting dad to come running out and kill us all stone dead. Nothing happened, he hadn't heard the bang, we had time to think. What could we say that would have the best outcome? Should I say I'd done it to save my mum? Bravery has never been one of my strong points, and after all, it wouldn't be the first time I'd damaged the car.

I'd got off lightly last time, did I really want to risk it a second time? Should we throw ourselves on his mercy and beg his forgiveness? How silly! Mercy and forgiveness weren't in dad's vocabulary. We couldn't think of anything so we decided to say nothing, and when he finally came out of the house we stood in front of the car door hiding the damage.

We got into the car and went on our way, I swear you could hear everyone's heart beating on the journey. If dad noticed we were unusually quiet he never said anything. He was probably just enjoying the peace and quiet instead of the usual argy bargy.

When we got to our destination dad got out and went around to the passenger side before we could stop him. He saw the damage. "God Jesus!" He said. "Look at me car." Time stood still again. We were paralysed with fear for a few moments before our survival instincts kicked in, then we all said in unison, "Oh my God! How did that happen?"

"I know who did it," he said.

Once again time stood still. "I bet it was that bastard who always parks next to me outside the pub. Wait till I see him!" We could breathe again. We never did tell him what really happened.

Memories

Memories are bittersweet,
they are the friends you love to meet.
They keep you sane, they cause you pain,
but still you visit time and again.

Sometimes were sad, but joys you had,
not all your memories were bad.
Loved ones past are waiting there,
visit them often, show them you care.

Remember your life and the gift that it was.
Don't shut it out, and think just because
it wasn't the life that you hoped it would be.
It was yours, it was precious, search your memory,
you'll see.

5. THE ORPHANAGE

I'd like to know if my dad ever thought back to the time when I was his favourite. He would sit me on the bathroom sink when I was small so I could watch him shave. When he'd finished he would take the blade out of his razor and let me have a go. I couldn't wait to grow up and have real bristles on my face and be able to shave properly just like him. Thank God that never happened!

All children want to be the favourite and when there are six of you it becomes even more important, and harder to obtain. It's not easy to get noticed, you can get lost in the crowd.

Being the favourite didn't manifest itself into extra sweet rations or less hidings, it was just an understanding, a special feeling. If you've never had it you spend your whole life chasing it. If you've always had it and it's taken away, you feel betrayed.

The first time I felt betrayed by my dad I was six years old. It was unwarranted as it turned out, but I didn't know it at the time.

It was a Sunday evening and everything was the same as every other Sunday except there seemed to be a bit of a festive atmosphere. It might have been someone's birthday. Aunty Betty was coming for tea which wasn't unusual, and mum was upstairs running the bath for us three girls.

I had no idea of the horror about to unfold.

I discovered a lovely big cake sitting on the sideboard in the kitchen and called my sister Catherine to come and have a look. "You won't be having any of that," she said. "Shurrup you!" I said, "Why not?" "Because you won't be here," she said and ran off. Why would she say that I wondered, but then I decided she was just being mean as usual, although there did seem to be something going on, no-one would look at me, I started to feel uneasy.

The evening carried on as normal. All three of us youngest girls got into the bath and a week's worth of dirt was scrubbed off. The tide marks around our necks were finally dealt to. So far so good, my fears began to subside, Catherine was obviously just making it up. I got out of the bath, dried myself off and started putting my pajamas on, but mum told me to get dressed. I noticed she'd laid out my best clothes, this had never happened before, we never went out at night. I didn't want to do it but I had to as I was told.

Once I was dressed she said, "Come on we have to go." She put my coat and shoes on me and we left the house. I didn't notice the suitcase in her hand.

We got on one bus and then another. I didn't ask where we were going, I already knew. There were too many children in our house, they needed to get rid of one so they'd chosen me.

I wasn't the baby anymore, I'd been replaced by my baby sister. I sat quietly looking out of the window thinking about all the bad things I'd done. Too late to be sorry now! If only dad had been home and not in the pub, I was sure he wouldn't have let her take me away. Who would make him laugh if I wasn't there?

It was dark when we finally arrived at the orphanage. I couldn't have imagined a scarier looking place. We went inside to a huge cold empty foyer and a lady in uniform came to meet us. Mum handed the suitcase to her and we were taken into a room off to one side. I was weighed and measured. I remember the lady saying, "Three feet tall and three stone…very good." Mum looked pleased when she heard that.

I was taken away then. There were no goodbye hugs or kisses. The lady took me into another room, inside were four of the biggest baths I'd ever seen. She turned the taps on one of the baths and just covered the bottom with cold water and said, "Get undressed and get in." I was horrified. "I've just had a bath, I don't need another one," I said. Two baths in one night, it was bad enough having to have one once a week. She was having none of that. She took my clothes off, put me into the bath and left the room.

It was cold and very scary being left in that room all by myself. I'd never been in a bath on my own before. there was always Catherine down the plug end, me at the other end, and my little sister Jayne in the middle.

The bath was so big I couldn't see over the sides, not that I wanted to. I just sat there shivering. After a few minutes the lady came back, lifted me out, dried me off, and gave me a pair of my own pajamas to put on. It was comforting having something familiar to wear in that horrible place.

I was led down a long corridor then through wide double doors with windows at the top. I was pleasantly surprised to find myself in a big, bright, cheerful room. A group of kids was sitting on cushions on the floor in one corner watching telly. There was a row of iron beds down one side of the room, and cots full of babies at the end. I was told to go and sit with the other kids. It might not be so bad after all if we were allowed to watch telly I thought.

I'd only just sat down when a voice said, "Ok kids lights out, everyone into bed." Another lady in uniform took me to my bed and the lights went out. I was scared then. I wanted to be in my own bedroom with my sisters. I wanted my dad to grab me and rub his raspy chin on my face, then carry me 'up the dancers' to bed like he did every night. I didn't even get to say goodbye to him. Did he know where I'd gone? Did he even notice I was missing?

I went straight to sleep, it had been a long day. Sometime in the night, I was woken by two women in uniforms dragging me out of bed. One of them pulled my pajamas off, slapped me on the leg and called me a 'dirty bitch.' I'd wet the bed.

"Get to the toilet." One of the women said. I didn't know where the toilet was so I just stood there. She pointed to a door at the end of the room and gave me a shove. I went through the door into a long dark corridor. I couldn't see any sign of a toilet, and I wasn't about to go looking in the dark, so I just waited for a few minutes then went back into the room. One of the women gave me some orphanage pyjamas to wear and put me back into bed.

I woke up the next morning ready to start my new life as an orphan. I didn't know what to expect, but was pleasantly surprised when I got breakfast in bed. No one told me to get up, so I lay there watching the hive of activity going on around me.

There were lots more kids than I'd seen the night before, and all the babies were crying. I felt sorry for them, at least I was a big girl, I was sure I could cope with my new situation.

The girl in the next bed smiled at me. I smiled back, might as well make friends if I was staying. She came over to talk to me. I thought she was brave getting out of bed without asking permission. I asked her how long she'd been at the orphanage. She looked a bit puzzled, then told me we were actually in Alder Hey Children's Hospital. She was one of those kids that know everything. "You're probably having your tonsils out like me," she said. "All the tonsils get taken out on Tuesday mornings."

I didn't know what tonsils were, I didn't care, I just knew that if this was a hospital and not an orphanage, I would get to go home.

The day of the operation arrived and the nurses brought round some funny little gowns for us to put on. They were very short and only came to my waist, so I left my knickers on. The know-all girl in the next bed said we weren't allowed to wear our knickers. I knew I would fight to the death if they tried to take them off me. Mum always told us, "Don't be showing all you've got." That advice has always stood me in good stead. I was so glad I left them on as they wheeled me out on a trolley without covering me up. The corridor was full of people, men in white coats, visitors coming to see their children. They all looked pityingly at me, probably trying to imagine what sort of terrible illness I had. They didn't have to feel sorry for me, I had my knickers on, all was right with the world.

I thought that right up until I got into the operating theatre and a giant needle was plunged into the veins in my wrist. My screams bounced off the walls and echoed around the room, gradually fading away as I went under the anaesthetic.

Mum came to visit a few days after the operation. She brought me a cake which I couldn't eat because my throat was so sore, and some Lucozade which was stolen out of my locker before I got to taste it. She also brought my brother John. He wasn't allowed in.

He was sixteen at the time but still classed as a child, and there were no children allowed to visit in a children's hospital. Undeterred, he climbed up the drainpipe outside and pulled faces at me through the window. He was a welcome sight.

Dad never came to see me in the hospital. I shouldn't be surprised about that. When John was thirteen he was in hospital for three months with rheumatic fever, dad never visited him once. I find it so hard to believe, but then we never expected dad to do normal Father things. We expected nothing from him, and that's exactly what we got.

He never came to see me in the hospital, but he hadn't betrayed me after all and went back to being my hero for a little while longer. He was wobbling on his pedestal for a few more years before he eventually fell off.

The Orphanage

Too many children, someone had to go,
which one to choose, eeny, meeny, miny, mo.
Was it really that random how they picked me
in my frightened child's mind that's what I see.

Imagination so vivid it was quick to take hold,
when they made the decision I was not to be told.
How could they not tell me, put my mind at rest,
I'd be gone a few days, a week at best.

Getting darker and darker, lights flashing by,
as I sit on the bus trying not to cry.
I want to be home, I don't want to go,
away from my family and all that I know.

6. RELUCTANT FATHER

I was born the fifth of six children to an Irish Catholic father, and a Welsh Protestant mother. Dad moved to England from Ireland when he was nineteen and joined the Royal Air Force, where he met my mum. They married in Gloucester Cathedral in January 1948.

It sounds quite grand getting married in a Cathedral, but it wasn't, there was just the two of them, two witnesses and a priest. No white dress, no flowers, and no photographer. I'd like to have seen a photograph of them on their wedding day. Maybe it would have shown if dad was happy, or feeling trapped by circumstance. Mum was pregnant.

Mum was dumped in a room somewhere after the wedding while dad went off to get drunk on their wedding night. Unfortunately that set the scene for their next fifty-nine years together.

Why they thought a bog Irish Catholic and a fairly well to do Welsh Protestant would have anything in common and be able to have a happy marriage is beyond me. It seems the families on both sides agreed and were disappointed in the match. I'm sure dad's parents were hoping for a fine young Irish girl, or at the very least a Catholic.

Mum did become a Catholic so she was allowed to get married in a church, but she was never a convert. I didn't know you could become a Catholic, I thought it was something you were born into, like your skin.

Mum and dad left the RAF after they got married, and with a baby in tow traveled around England and Ireland looking for work. The reality of family life in the early days was tough. No jobs to be found, no money for food, and more mouths to feed every year.

They were thrown out of their first accommodation when the landlady found out mum was pregnant. She'd spotted the milkman delivering free orange juice to their door, all pregnant women were entitled to it after the war.

Their first Christmas together was a miserable affair. They already had one baby and there was another on the way. They'd managed to find somewhere to live, but it was just one room at the top of a boarding house. Dad hadn't been able to get any work so they had no money, and no food. They didn't have much furniture and had to sit on orange crates which left mum with a lifetime obsession with buying chairs.

When I told her once I was going on holiday to Fiji she said it was a waste of money. "What will you have to show for it when you come back, you could buy a chair with that money," she said. "I'll have nice memories" I replied. "Well, you can't sit on them, can you?" She said.

A parcel arrived from Ireland just in time for their first Christmas dinner. It was a freshly killed chicken from dad's family in Ireland. Unfortunately, after a week in the post it wasn't quite so fresh anymore. Mum cried. If only they'd sent a tin of beans.

You could argue their circumstances would drive a man to drink, but drink was a luxury dad couldn't afford. He didn't always see it that way though.

They say, 'what doesn't kill you makes you stronger.' But if you turn to alcohol for your strength then you just get weaker, and those around you suffer for your weakness.

After a few nomadic years they eventually settled in Liverpool in 1950. I arrived in 1960, exactly two years after my sister Catherine. Not many people know this, but I was a donor baby, probably the world's first. I wasn't conceived for my body parts as you might imagine, just for my company. There weren't any kindergartens or play-centres at the time Catherine was born, and the worry was that she wouldn't have anyone to play with when the older kids were at school. I console myself with the fact that I was probably the only one of the six children who was planned and wanted, if not for the right reasons. But still, I can't help wondering if I would be here today if there had been a little girl living next door for Catherine to play with.

I was born at home with all the older kids waiting in the next room. Dad was in the pub 'wetting the baby's head.' There was always a free drink on offer for the new father. So if nothing else, having all those babies gave him a good excuse for a drink, not that he ever needed one. But every new baby born was another mouth to feed, and potentially one less drink to be had. I think he resented us for that.

There was a six-year age gap between the first three children and the second three, so we were like two separate families. The first three children were born close together. Rosaleen, also known as 'Posy' was born five months after mum and dad got married. Mum was naïve. Dad told her she couldn't get pregnant unless they used 'the instrument.' When the doctor announced a baby was on the way, mum said, "I can't be pregnant, we didn't use the instrument." A quick lesson about the birds and the bees followed, but it obviously didn't sink in, John was born fifteen months later.

Kevin arrived two years after John. Dad wasn't usually around when the babies were being born, but he was there when Kevin arrived. He had to give the midwife a good telling off because she gave mum a slap. Dad always told the joke about how the baby was so ugly the midwife slapped the mother, but I'm sure that's not what happened in this case.

Catherine arrived after a break of six years, unplanned and unwanted like all the others. There wasn't a lot of choice in those days.

Dad didn't accept Catherine was his baby for the first few years of her life. He and mum had separated briefly before she was conceived, and he always said mum only came back because she was pregnant. He wouldn't have anything to do with Catherine, mum wasn't even allowed to feed her in his presence. "You're not wasting my hard-earned money feeding someone else's bastard" he'd say.

Once I was born and started to grow, Catherine and I looked so much alike, mum thought dad couldn't ignore the fact she must be his. Nevertheless, I can remember him being mean to her when I was little and not knowing why. I'd feel sorry for her when she would do the same things I did to get his attention, and he would just ignore her, or tell her to "Get lost." He could be so cruel.

Catherine grew tall, and it wasn't long before she was towering over him. It's hard for a girl to be too tall, but dad didn't make any concessions. "Get out of me way ye big ugly thing ye." He would say to her. Self-esteem was in short supply at our house.

I hope dad came to appreciate her towards the end of his life, because out of all of us, I think she loved him the most.

So for a while I was the baby of the family. I was the apple of my dad's eye, and with four older brothers and sisters I was spoilt rotten, and I liked it. But when I was three life as I knew it changed forever.

One morning I came downstairs and went into the kitchen. I was shocked to see dad wearing my mum's pink candlewick dressing gown. He was busy making breakfast, porridge with salt, no sugar. He didn't believe in putting sugar on porridge, which was the only thing that made it edible in my opinion.

Now this day and age you might be thinking about a completely different scenario if you saw your Father dressing in your mum's clothes, but I just thought mum had died in the night, and no one had bothered to tell me. I asked dad where mum was and he said those terrible words no child ever wants to hear. "She's gone to the hospital to get a new baby." I was shocked! Why do they need a new baby when they have me I thought? Wasn't I good enough? Why had no one told me mum was getting a baby? Who knew baby sisters could just arrive seemingly out of nowhere, whether you liked it or not. I didn't!

Later that day dad went off to the hospital to pick up mum and the new baby. I waited in the hallway by the front door all day, I wanted to see this thing that was taking my place.

Eventually dad arrived home. He came in the door and ran straight upstairs. I asked him where the baby was. "She's in here," he said, holding up a suitcase. I was so pleased, I thought he can't like her very much if he's stuck her in a suitcase.

My happiness was short-lived. Mum came in holding the new bundle of joy. So that was that! I moved up a rung in the ladder of life. I wasn't the baby anymore.

I thought my relationship with my dad would change once there was a new baby to play with, but it didn't. I don't ever remember having to compete for his attention when I was little. Just as well, that sort of thing can scar a person for life, and there was more than enough scarring to be done later on.

And so my dad became the reluctant father of six children, starting at the tender age of twenty-two. Little did he know he would have to put up with at least one of them in his house for the next thirty-six years. I think he would have headed for the hills if he'd known, that's more than most fathers have to endure. Mind you, some fathers might not see it as an endurance test.

So maybe he could be forgiven for standing up at my wedding and saying, "I've waited twenty-three years to get rid of her, you've taken the whore of me hands." That was just before he started singing, 'My Wild Irish Rose.' My shame was complete. Funnily enough, I just remember being pleased and surprised that he knew how old I was. I don't know if that's any worse than what he said when Rosaleen got married for the second time. Dad walked her towards the celebrant and said in a big loud voice, "I hope this is the last time. Who do you think you are? Elizabeth Taylor?"

Reluctant Father

He never wanted six, he never wanted any,
one by one they all arrived, why did he have so many?

Never enough money, never enough food,
how did he cope with such a brood?

He turned his back, drank heavily,
it came to him so easily.

He should have stopped, he should have paused,
could he not see the pain it caused.

Can we forgive, can we not say,
we love you dad in our own way.

No need to hang your head in shame,
we love you still, that's why we came.

And at the end, all six were there,
but much too late to show we care.

7. BIG FAMILY

ROSALEEN

I'd like to say we were one big happy family, and it certainly felt that way when I was a small child. It was great having so many big brothers and sisters, there was always something going on and always someone to play with. Our house was full of noise, music, fighting, arguing and laughing, but not when dad was home. Then we would tiptoe around being careful not to laugh, or talk too loud, and God help us if we ran up and down the stairs.

It was Rosaleen's job to look after all five of us in the evenings while mum was at work and dad was in the pub. Naturally, she resented us, she just wanted a normal life like any other teenager. Her freedom became more and more elusive as each new baby came along. She was twelve when I was born, and fifteen by the time the youngest, was born.

I don't remember the resentment, I just remember the fun times, and the bedtime stories she told us every night. The long-running saga of Mr. and Mrs. Moth who lived in the airing cupboard. She made it up as she went along, she was a great storyteller.

One night she came in late, lit the old gas fire on the bedroom wall and got us three girls up out of bed. We sat around the fire on the floor while she told us the next instalment of the Moth family.

It was magic, a million miles away from sitting around a campfire, but similar all the same.

It was a sad day when Rosaleen left home at eighteen. No more stories! I used to check the airing cupboard every now and then to see if Mr. and Mrs. Moth were still in there, but I never saw them.

Rosaleen came back for a visit after she got married and announced one morning she was taking us to the beach in her new car. We ran around excitedly collecting buckets and spades and swimming costumes, we even made sandwiches for the journey. We never left the driveway. It seems she hadn't learned how to drive yet. We managed to enjoy the imaginary sun, surf, and sand, but the imaginary ice-cream was a bit of a stretch.

Rosaleen didn't have any privacy, she had to share her bedroom with her three little sisters until she left home. Her bed was under the window and there was just a white fluffy rug and a dressing table separating her bed from ours. That was her domain and she guarded it fiercely, we weren't allowed into her space. She would check the rug every day to see if there were any tell-tale footprints on it. But we were smarter than that. We would always shake out the rug after we'd been jumping on her bed, and rifling through her drawers to see what we could find.

The bane of Rosaleen's' life was her name. It was shortened to 'Rosie Posy' when she was a baby, and 'Posy' stuck.

One day, deciding she'd suffered enough, she pinned us up against the wall one by one and threatened us within an inch of our lives if she ever heard us calling her 'Posy' again. She put the fear of God into us and I swear I have never used that name to this day. Honest!

Rosaleen took tap dancing lessons and would come home and teach us her routines, whether we wanted to learn or not. When dad came home late at night from the pub bringing with him whatever 'derelicts' he'd found there, we'd be dragged out of bed, lined up, still in our nightdresses, and made to perform for them. The Von Trapp family of Liverpool!

The old drunks would give us money. I hated it, but it was very lucrative. I had a particularly prosperous evening one night and my money box was full. My brother John very kindly offered to look after it for me in case I lost it. I never saw it again.

Rosaleen thought Catherine and I should learn to play the piano but mum said it was a waste of money. "It'll be a five-minute wonder" she'd say. So Rosaleen paid for our lessons out of her own money.

Just before she left home to go to Canada for a year, Rosaleen decided it was high time Catherine and I learned about the birds and the bees. I was only seven and more than happy with the explanation I'd been given about babies being found in a cabbage patch. Undeterred, she sat us down, got out a pen and paper, and drew a diagram of the underside of a rabbit. She kept asking if we understood what she was saying. We kept nodding, and trying to look interested. When she'd finished she said, "Well, did you understand that?" We nodded. "Do you have any questions?" We shook our heads. "Good," she said and went off looking pleased with herself. I looked at Catherine, she looked at me. "Any idea what all that was about?" I said. "I think we're getting a rabbit," said Catherine.

When Rosaleen got back from Canada she was horrified to find we were still sleeping with the light on. Mum and dad were out every night and we were scared being in the house on our own in the dark. We had gotten into the habit of leaving the light on and mum would turn it off when she came home at nine-thirty. Rosaleen was having none of that. She turned the light off and closed the door, but pretty soon the sound of our crying brought her back in. She sat on the bed in the dark with us and told us to wait. A car came down the street and illuminated the room with its headlights. "See" she said, "If you're scared you just have to wait for another car." We were happy with that, not realising we were on a back road with very little traffic. We fell asleep waiting for another car that never came.

Nevertheless, to this day when I'm on my own at night and hear a car coming down the road I remember that night, and feel a great sense of comfort.

Rosaleen got married to her first husband when I was eight. It was the biggest event of my life so far and very exciting. I was to be one of six bridesmaids. We wore long blue satin dresses with little puff sleeves made by a real dressmaker, not just mum who usually made our clothes. I don't think anyone had taken into consideration the fact that the wedding was in November and it was going to be freezing. A sleeveless satin dress is not the best thing to be wearing on a cold winter's day.

The temperature kept dropping, and it was obvious it was going to snow. Mum raced into town and came back with a bolt of white needlecord. She spent hours sewing six capes, and muffs for us to wear. They weren't very warm, but they kept the hypothermia at bay in the freezing cold church. The Catholic ceremony took over an hour.

The wedding was at eleven in the morning so we had to get our hair done the day before. It was my first time at the hairdresser's, mum had always cut our hair. I was left under the dryer too long and fainted, I was told off by everyone for causing a fuss. My long hair was put up in a bun and studded with tiny blue rosebuds. The elaborate hair-do had to stay intact until the next day, so can after can of hair spray was applied to all the bridesmaids.

If you've ever wondered when the hole in the ozone first appeared, it was November the fifth, nineteen sixty-eight. Mum covered my head with a scarf that night and put me to bed with strict instructions not to move.

We had the most beautiful shoes to wear. They were beige patent leather with a T-bar strap and little heels. I'd come home from school every day, put them on and clip-clop around the bedroom. I could do that because we didn't have any carpet, just freezing cold Lino.

A few days before the wedding everything went still, the sky went pink, and down came the snow. There is nothing more magical than snow falling out of a night sky. Catherine and I watched out of the bedroom window and prayed for it not to stop. It's not that we wanted to spoil the wedding, we had a hidden agenda. When it snowed and got thick on the ground, all the kids in the street would come out and turn the road into an ice rink. We would slide and skate for hours. When a car came down the road we would dive behind a hedge and watch as it skidded around the corners.

We only had a short time to skate because the salt trucks would come in the night and melt the snow, we would be left with wet dirty slush for days on end. The snow settled. Dad put us to bed at the usual time, drinking time. We waited for him to leave for the pub, then we got dressed and sneaked out of the house.

There we were all lined up with the other kids of the neighbourhood ready to slide to our hearts' content, but we found the tread on our shoes was too thick. Mum always insisted on buying us boys' brogues because they lasted longer. They sure did, no amount of abuse could wear them out. I was so embarrassed having to wear them to school that I used to stand up against the wall with one leg up behind me like an ostrich. I thought it wouldn't be so bad if the other kids could only see one shoe at a time. My friends would come up and ask me to come and play, but I'd say, "No, I'm ok standing here thanks."

So anyway, this night we were faced with a dilemma, we didn't have any other shoes. Or did we? Catherine came up with one of her 'Brilliant Ideas.' "The Wedding Shoes," She said. I recoiled in horror. "No, they'll get ruined," I said. "Knowing my luck I'll break a heel off or something. She said she was prepared to take the risk. I didn't want to be left out so against my better judgment I went and put mine on too. They were the best sliding shoes ever because the soles were nice and smooth.

We stayed out skating and sliding as long as we could, it was great fun. By the time mum and dad came home at nine-thirty we were safely tucked up in bed. The wedding shoes were dried off, shined up, and put back in their boxes. No damage done, no one ever found out. Until now!

Unfortunately the Wedding day ended in tears like all our family occasions. Uncle Tommy had a few too many and upset the groom by getting up on stage and grabbing the microphone. He wanted to sing 'Nobody's Child' and have everyone in tears like all good Irish shindigs.

So while I was tucked up in bed, exhausted from a long eventful day, the adults in my family were brawling in the street like tinkers.

Rosaleen was a bit like a drill sergeant for most of my early years. She had us hup-two-ing every weekend cleaning up our room, which we hated doing. But she was there for me at some difficult times in my life.

When I was ten she was home for a visit and found me crying into my pillow because I'd passed the Eleven Plus exam. She couldn't understand how passing an exam could be the cause of such misery, but passing meant going to a grammar school where I knew no-one. Failing the exam meant going to the local high school with all my friends. I was more than happy to go to the local high school, I didn't have any lofty ambitions. I made the mistake of telling mum I wanted to work in the bra factory across the road when I left school. If I'd tried really hard I couldn't have said a worse thing, she went mad. Her reaction took me completely by surprise and it made me think maybe I should set my sights a little higher. If she believed I was destined for greater things, who was I to argue.

I didn't believe it though, I suspected mum was just trying to keep up with the Jones's. All my life my cousin Debbie, mum's only niece who was a year younger than me, had been held up as a shining example of what a child could achieve. Mum would say, "Debbie's passed this exam, Debbie's teaching piano and she's only fourteen, Debbie's going to university to be a doctor." How was I supposed to compete with that? It didn't spur me on, it just made me jealous of her. After all, she was an only child, the odds were already stacked in her favour, what chance did I have as a fifth child. That sort of achievement is the result of time spent with parents nurturing and encouraging. I didn't even get picked up from school on my first day, they forgot about me. Luckily I'd learned my address off by heart and was pointed in the right direction by the lollypop man who found me on the corner looking forlorn.

My jealousy reached new heights every Christmas when Debbie got sent the best present. For years I'd been asking for a toy baby grand piano. I'd leave the catalogue open at the toy section with my wish list circled. I came home from school early one day a few weeks before Christmas and there was the baby grand piano on the kitchen table, I was overjoyed to say the least. I ran back out of the door thinking mum had forgotten to hide it, and if she knew I'd seen it she wouldn't give it to me.

I must admit there was a niggling doubt in the back of my mind, I couldn't understand why she'd left it there in full view when she knew I was due home. Mum was the master hider of presents, as hard as we tried over the years, we never found her secret stash.   Eventually I had to go inside and when mum saw me she said, "Oh look what I've bought Debbie for Christmas."

Rosaleen convinced me what a great opportunity it was going to grammar school, and told me how proud everyone was that I'd passed the test, the only one in the   family to do so. I was very grateful, no-one had ever taken the time to talk to me like that before. When I'd been upset about something I was always told to 'grow up,' or 'don't be such a big baby.' Rosaleen said it would be great, and I would soon make new friends.

She was right of course. And I must say it was nice being in a different school from the rest of my siblings, and not being compared to Catherine every day. One teacher at junior school called me Catherine for a whole year, and would get annoyed when I didn't respond, but I never knew she was talking to me. She never got tired of saying, "Oh that's right you're Suzanne, not as clever as your sister are you?"

There was a list of schools to choose from, so thinking I wouldn't be lucky enough to get my first, or second choice, I put my favourite one down third. 'Everton Valley,' it had such a nice ring to it. I put my least favourite first 'Mary Help Of Christians' what a mouth full.

I ended up getting my first choice. I don't know why I was making such monumental decisions that could change my whole life by myself, I was only eleven. There might have been a bit of coercion from mum. I found out later that Rosaleen's sister-in-law went to the same school and there were hand me down uniforms to be had.

I used to joke that dad never even knew what school I went to. We had a bit of a family get-together a few years later and someone mentioned the Eleven Plus exam. "Well, none of you lot passed" he said. "I did!" I said. "Well, that's the first I've heard of it," he replied. It doesn't always feel good to be proved right.

I went to live with Rosaleen and her family when I was sixteen. It was a nice period in my life… peaceful. There was no more fighting and arguing. I had my own space, and freedom to come and go as I pleased. Moving out of home wasn't a popular decision, I was working by then so my board money came in handy. The day I left I was told in no uncertain terms not to darken their doorstep again, which I had no intention of doing.

But circumstances change, and after a while I had to reluctantly leave Rosaleen's house. My brother-in-law came into my bedroom one night and I knew I couldn't stay there any longer. I had nowhere else to go except back home, but I couldn't tell them the reason because I didn't want to cause any trouble.

I enlisted the help of Catherine after swearing her to secrecy. She paved the way for me and set up a meeting with 'the parents.' It was like going for a job interview. I was sitting opposite them while Catherine pleaded my case. Dad held his tongue for a while, but then he couldn't help himself. "Coming crying back to daddy are ye, can't make it on yer own eh!" It was humiliating, but I still didn't tell him the real reason. If I had I know he would have welcomed me back with open arms, but at what cost to the family. He kept on and on until mum saw that I was getting upset and told him to shut up, then she said I could come home.

I wasn't there long, Catherine decided we should move into a flat together. We had no furniture, no telephone, no car, and neither of us could cook, but we didn't care, we were free at last. We ran down the front path laughing with these words ringing in our ears, "You leave this house don't think you can come swanning back in when it suits you."

It was only a few months before I was back home again, I never stayed away for long, which is probably what prompted dad's little speech at my wedding. He didn't think I was ever going to stay away for good. Even after I was married I went to stay with him for six weeks with my first baby. My husband was away on a course, and I didn't want to stay home alone, but dad thought I'd left him, and wasn't letting on.

Every time I looked up I'd catch him staring at me, he was trying to read my mind and find out the truth. It was possibly one of the happiest days of his life when my husband came to take me and the baby home.

Anyway having a big sister came in handy over the years, and none more so than when dad went into the Rest-home. I was so glad she was with me, I would hate to have had to go through something like that on my own. There were some perks to not being an only child after all.

Rosaleen taught me many things over the years. How to cook and sew, how to clean the house, and how to put on makeup. She was the one who lent me a dress and waited up for me when I went on my first date.

She also taught me the most important lesson a girl needs to carry her through life.

Moisturise!

JOHN

Dad said John was born trouble. He said he'd had to nail his cot to the floor when he was a toddler because he would rock back and forth so violently the cot would move from one end of the room to the other.

Every morning John would watch with interest as dad put Brylcreem on his hair to keep it in check. Dad went into John's room one morning and found him with his hand down his nappy, scooping up quantities of a certain substance he'd found in there, and plastering it on his head. Just like his dad eh!

John was my hero, he was as mad as a meat axe, but lots of fun. On Christmas mornings he would come into our room to see what Father Christmas had left at the end of our bed. He'd find the best toy and say, "I bought you that." I believed him, I thought he was the best brother in the world.

He surprised us one day when he came down the stairs dressed in Rosaleen's best clothes. Stockings, suspender belt, high heels, and make-up. "Come on girls we're going into town on the bus," he said, in a suitably high pitched voice. As young as I was I knew that wasn't such a good idea. Fortunately we only got as far as the staircase, our imaginary bus. John sat up the front pointing out the sights looking for all the world like Mrs. Doubtfire.

Our John was what you might call a borrower. If you had something he wanted he would say, "You're not using this are ye?" Or, "You don't need that do ye?" You couldn't say no to him he was such a charmer. He got the contents of my money box on more than one occasion.

When he was a teenager he was caught stealing a box of matches from the local shop. The police brought him home. Dad was livid, he took his belt off and gave John the hiding of his life. I was surprised, I honestly thought he would just tell him to be more careful next time, meaning don't get caught! Like I said kids do learn by example. Anyway, it was all a bit of a joke being caught stealing a box of matches, if they'd only known about all the other things he'd stolen over the years. John was a real'Artful Dodger. He wore an overcoat to school with big pockets on the inside. We would put our order in for chalk, pencils, or books, and he would always oblige.

One day dad took John with him to see the parish priest, he needed money and thought the church would help him, especially if he had a little boy in tow. He was given his marching orders once again. So John went to church the following week and stole all the money out of the collection plate.

When I wouldn't let John ride the new bike I got for my fifth birthday he slashed all the tyre's with his penknife.

I'm not complaining, it was the ugliest bike I'd ever seen. For a start it was a three-wheeler, I mean come on, I was five, I was starting school soon, I didn't need a three-wheeler. It had a compartment on the back that you could open and put stuff in. What stuff? I didn't have any stuff. But worst of all there was a handle underneath that you could pull out. It was a training handle. Actually, that wasn't the worst thing. The worse thing was that it was made of tin and it rattled and banged as I cycled along the road, you could hear me coming for miles.

I know mum did her best, I can still see her face when she brought it out to show me, she was so pleased with her red paint job. Yes, It was second hand. I tried to look happy, and even took it for a ride, but I could hear the sniggers from the kids in the street. So I was glad when John slashed the tyres, I thought I'd finally get the two-wheeler with the little basket on the front, and the little bell on the handlebars I'd been dreaming about for so long. Tring! Tring! I never did.

More disturbingly John would hold a three-year-old Jayne by the ankles and dip her head into the fishpond in the back garden. Other times he would press her flat up against the ceiling until she was screaming. I always wanted to help her but I knew he would only do it to me instead and I think I already mentioned I was a bit of a coward.

Then there was the incident with the air rifle, but luckily no one was hurt.

John got the gun to shoot the pigeons on the neighbour's roof. They would fly in his bedroom window and roost on his top bunk bed. He was never meant to sit at the window like a sniper threatening to shoot anyone who came near the front gate.

John was always bringing home injured, or abandoned animals. Pigeons with broken wings, hedgehogs he'd rescued from the road. One day he brought home a tortoise. We called him 'Fred,' and painted his name in white paint on his shell. We'd tie a piece of string around his neck and take him for walks. Needless to say, it was a slow journey and we didn't get very far.

We found out tortoises hibernate in the winter so we put him in a shoebox and buried him in the garden. When we dug him up some months later there was just an empty shell. I think we got hibernating, and burying alive mixed up.

When John came home with his first pair of jeans we watched in fascination as he put them on, filled the bath full of water and got in. We thought it was another one of his antics to make us laugh, but he told us he was trying to shrink them, and make them into stovepipes.

I don't know if he was a 'Mod' or a 'Rocker,' but he did pick me up from school one day on a motor scooter. I felt so proud, until he took off too fast and I wasn't holding on properly so I fell off in the middle of the road in front of all my school friends.

I have a faint scar on my left hand to remind me of John. Sometimes he was left in charge of us little ones in the evenings. He didn't take his responsibilities very seriously and we were left to our own devices most of the time.

One night John built a go-cart using the wheels off our old pram. It was very impressive, except in mum's eyes, as she hadn't actually said he could have the pram. She was probably hoping to sell it, or God forbid, keep it for yet another baby.

John charged all the kids in the street a penny a ride. I asked him if I could have a ride too and he said, "Have you got a penny?" I didn't, so the answer was "No."

The evening wore on and I got hungry so I went outside and asked him to come in and cut me a slice of bread. He said I'd have to wait because he was too busy. I didn't want to wait, so I went into the kitchen and climbed up onto a chair. The loaf of bread was sitting in its usual place on the breadboard on the kitchen table. I picked up the knife and started to cut. I didn't realise I was cutting my hand until I saw the bread turn red. I started screaming.

John came running in. When he saw what I'd done he knew he was in big trouble if mum found out, so he stopped the bleeding, cleaned me up, and destroyed all the evidence. He said if I promised not to tell mum or dad he would let me ride in his go-cart.

I had pride of place in the front seat of his go-cart for the rest of the evening. It nearly cost me my hand, but it didn't cost me a penny.

John was thrown out of the house when he was sixteen. Dad had ordered him not to come home until he'd had a haircut, a proper one, short back and sides. John had been growing his hair for a while trying to achieve the Beatles long haircut of the day. We'd watch him standing in front of the mirror in the kitchen cabinet, combing it down over his forehead, then shaking his head like Paul McCartney used to do.

He didn't get the haircut, and so he had a bad feeling on his way home from work that day. As the bus pulled up to his stop he found he didn't want to get off. He stayed on until the bus came round to his stop again, he had to get off eventually, he couldn't escape the inevitable.

Dad was sitting at the kitchen table when he walked in the back door, John could see he was drunk. Dad took one look at him, still with his long hair, and took off his belt. John ran upstairs to his bedroom with dad chasing after him, and mum chasing after both of them.

John tried to get out of the window, but he couldn't fit. Dad came in and started thrashing the life out of him with the belt. Mum was behind him screaming for dad to leave him alone. John was bigger than dad by this time, so when the beating didn't stop, he mustered all his strength and pushed him in the chest.

Dad fell backward into the old oak wardrobe and landed heavily on the base, it broke, and dad got stuck in it so John was able to make his escape. He ran out of the house with dad's voice ringing in his ears, "Get out of my house," he yelled. "Get out and don't come back."

It sounds comical now but it was a terrifying moment, nothing like that had ever happened before, none of us had ever retaliated. All the fights had the same pattern so we always knew what to expect. Dad would get drunk, he'd started picking on someone, a fight would break out, we'd all run for cover, and whoever got caught would get a hiding. There's comfort in tradition, whatever that tradition may be.

I waited until it was safe to move then I ran after John. I can still hear my little six-year-old voice saying, "Where you going John?" "I'm getting out of here and I'm not coming back!" He said. I didn't know where he could go, but John had a contingency plan. He'd found a hostel in town where he could stay in an emergency, he knew it was only a matter of time before he'd have to leave, he couldn't take much more.

I couldn't imagine life without him, he brought so much fun into the house. I sat at the bottom of the stairs beside the front door for a long time hoping he would come back.

He did eventually come back months later, but he never lived with us again. He joined the Merchant Navy, then the Royal Air Force, and then got married. Like all of us, he could never stay away for long, and I was always happy to see his car parked outside the house when I came home from school.

When John left the Air force after a few years Catherine and I gave him a dishonourable discharge ceremony. I'm not saying he got a dishonourable discharge, but he did have a habit of forgetting to go back when he was home on leave. We pulled the buttons and insignia off his uniform whilst whistling an appropriate military tune. I was good at whistling.

We left England when I was fourteen and we left John behind.

Our John

So many years since we said goodbye,
seems like yesterday, doesn't time fly.
Maybe not for you, the one who was left,
I remember your face, shocked and bereft.

At the time of our leaving
just the start of your grieving.
Your whole family gone in the blink of an eye,
enough to make a grown man cry.

We sailed away full of excitement,
no thought for you, a sad indictment.
We did hope you'd come and join us one day,
but it never worked out, what a price to pay.

KEVIN

Our Kevin didn't like me very much. I don't blame him, it can't have been easy having three snotty-nosed little sisters trailing around after you all the time, especially when you have all the girls in the neighbourhood to impress. Still, that's no excuse for him leaving me on the bus, on purpose, I was only four.

One morning I overheard him asking Catherine if she would like to go to the pictures. I asked if I could go too but he said no. Mum overheard this, conversation and said her usual, "You can't take one without the other." Like we were a couple of bookends. I saw the look on Kevin's face and knew it didn't bode well for me. I quickly said, "It doesn't matter, I don't want to go." It was too late, mum had seen an opportunity for an afternoon of peace.

I was made to walk ten paces behind them all the way to the bus stop. They seemed to be walking faster, and faster, as if they were trying to lose me. Catherine kept turning around to make sure I was keeping up, she always looked out for me. We got on the bus and they sat together at the front, I was left to go down to the back by myself. Catherine told me to keep an eye on her and she would let me know when it was time to get off. Easier said than done, the bus was filling up and people were standing in the aisle obscuring my view.

When I couldn't see them anymore I started to get scared. Then I heard a knock on the window outside the bus. It was Catherine, she was waving frantically telling me to hurry up and get off. It was too late, the bus was already moving and I was too small to reach the bell. I jumped up and pushed my way down the aisle to the front of the bus. A lady told the driver to stop and let me off when she saw I had been left behind. I hopped down from the bus and ran after them sobbing my heart out. Kevin looked disappointed to see me. I never asked to go with them again.

Kevin was the hero of the hour when mum decided to take us to the Liverpool show. It was exciting we didn't go on many outings, well actually we didn't go on any. Six kids was a logistical nightmare, and dad was never around to help. There was no way he would waste valuable drinking time to be with us. Even many years later when I would drive three, four, six hours, depending on where I was living, to bring my children to visit, he would still go out at the witching hour and come home at the usual time, drunk. If the Queen herself was coming it wouldn't have made a difference to him.

So on this momentous outing to the Liverpool show there was just me, about nine years old, Catherine, Jayne, Kevin, and mum. We were late, and it was raining, so we ran all the way to the bus stop.

When we got to the top of the road we could see the bus was already pulling into the stop. "Hurry up, run, we can make it," Mum shouted. The bus was one of the old double-deckers with the open platform at the back, you could still hop on if it had started moving.

I was the last one to get on, but the platform was wet from the rain, so before I could grab onto the pole I slipped and fell off the bus. I landed with a thump in the middle of the road. I sat there winded, unable to move, with my eyes tight shut waiting to be run over. Nothing happened. I tentatively turned around to meet my fate. I was sitting in the middle of Muirhead Avenue, the main road leading into the city, and it was completely empty of traffick, it was a miracle! I crawled to the safety of the pavement and watched as the bus got further and further away. No Liverpool Show for me!

I sat there feeling sorry for myself, wondering what to do next, when I saw the bus stop. Kevin jumped off and came running towards me, then the others got off. I didn't expect them to come back for me, I was pleased. That was until I saw Jayne standing on the platform at the back of the bus as it drove away. They'd forgotten about her.

I waved frantically to get their attention before Jayne was lost forever. Kevin turned around and chased the bus all the way to the next stop to rescue her. We did make it to the show, but it was the first and last time we ever went.

Like John, Kevin was also an accomplished thief. He'd come home from school with wads of free bus tickets procured from the teacher's desk. They were great, if you didn't go the whole distance for the price of the ticket, the conductor would give you change.

I'm not even sure I should mention the 'Chain Gang'… but I will anyway.

The council was renovating the houses across the road from our house in Liverpool. They'd cleared all the tenants out and were giving the houses a complete overhaul. We were living in the middle of a building site for months. It was noisy and dusty, but it had its compensations for a couple of teenage girls in the form of some very nice, half-clad, young builders.

Mum wanted a new front path, and it just so happened that a pallet load of pavers had been delivered to the house across the road. A plan was hatched. Under cover of darkness, dad formed us all into a human chain gang stretching from our house, across the road, and into the garden where the pavers were just waiting to be liberated. Dad took the pavers off the pile one by one and handed them to Kevin. He handed them to Catherine, and she handed them to me. Mum was at the end of the chain carefully stacking them behind the garage out of sight.

It all went without a hitch, apart from a tense moment when a car came down the road and we all had to dive behind a hedge and wait till the coast was clear.

"Isn't this stealing?" I asked my dad as we were crouched in the undergrowth. "Not at all," he said. "The Corporation owns this house, and the government owns the Corporation. You can't steal from the government." That didn't sound very logical to me, but dad was Irish, logic wasn't his first language.

Some would say that this was downright theft, but this was Liverpool. It was common knowledge that if something wasn't nailed down, or locked away, it was there for the taking. If we hadn't taken them, someone else probably would have. Even so, it didn't sit well with me. I knew stealing was one of the ten deadly sins, and I wasn't looking forward to lying to the priest at confession that week.

No-one came looking for the stolen pavers so once the coast was clear mum and dad set about laying the new path. Mum was very pleased with the result.

Now I was taught in my fervent religious Catholic upbringing, that God is always watching, and bad deeds don't go unpunished. So it was no surprise to me when a few months later a pipe burst under the new path and it all had to be dug up.

I don't know if dad ever made it through the 'Pearly Gates,' but if the streets are paved with gold like they say, he might just organise another chain gang.

Kevin went to sea when he was sixteen, and after a few trips home from exotic places, at nineteen he went on his last trip and disappeared. All his belongings were sent home from his ship, and we were left to wait, and wonder what had happened to him.

A few months passed before we got a letter from him telling us he was alive and well, but that he could never come home. He'd jumped ship in New Zealand, changed his name, and was making a new life for himself over there. We were devastated, of course, knowing we might never see him again. But once it was confirmed he was never coming home, we were like a pack of vultures dividing his belongings amongst ourselves. There was a surprising amount of women's clothing in his suitcase. We figured there had to be a woman behind his monumental decision, there usually is. It was four years before we saw him again.

Many years later when dad died I asked Kevin if he would like to read the eulogy at the funeral. I knew what he would say even before I asked him. "I've got nothing nice to say about him." I understood that, because I felt exactly the same way. His relationship with dad, like all of ours, was a tenuous one, and I couldn't begin to explain it. But I do know when dad was having one of his hospital emergencies and was on life support, Kevin sat by his side holding his hand.

A few days after dad's recovery I went to visit him in hospital. "Kevin's coming in soon," I said to him. "I don't want him here, he tried to kill me," he said. I laughed remembering the day dad was hallucinating, trying to escape from his hospital bed. Even heavily sedated with morphine he still managed to make a nuisance of himself.

He struggled and fought to get off the bed. He'd had open-heart surgery and was in danger of opening his wound, so Kevin and I had to hold him down until the nurses could restrain him. He was very strong, we had to practically sit on him. I told dad about Kevin sitting with him for hours holding his hand, and that it was just the drugs making him think Kevin was trying to kill him. I'm not saying Kevin has never tried to kill him, he did try to run him over once after a particularly nasty fight, but on his occasion he was innocent.

CATHERINE

It's hard to talk about Catherine as a separate person because we were like twins. We looked alike, we were almost the same size, and we were dressed the same, much to her disgust. We did everything together, so she is in almost every memory. That's why, all through this book I talk about 'We,' not 'I'.

We shared the fun, the fear, the anger, and the hidings. She probably won't agree with me but she was the cause of many of those hidings. She always had some 'brilliant idea' she would insist I take part in.

We got our half-crowns from Uncle Tommy one day and Catherine said she was going to the chemist to buy some nail polish. Not to be outdone, even though as nine-year-old I would have preferred some Batman cards and bubble gum, I bought some too. Unbeknown to me Catherine bought a very pale pink, hardly noticeable on her fingernails. When I asked her if I should buy blood-red nail polish, she thought that was a 'brilliant idea.' I painted my nails, and most of my fingers, then went and showed the rest of the family. Mum went completely mad, threw my nail polish in the bin, and took the rest of the money off me. We didn't have any nail polish remover so she said I had to go to school like that and, "Wo betide you when the teacher sees those nails."

I spent the rest of the night trying to scrape it off.

It was Catherine's idea to collect hundreds of caterpillar eggs and bring them into the parlour so we could watch them hatch. We didn't know it would happen overnight and they'd be crawling all over the floor when mum got up the next morning. Hundreds of weapons of mass destruction making a beeline for her potted geraniums on the window sill. She showed no mercy, she hoovered them all up, we couldn't save them.

Catherine told me if I cut the hair of my favourite doll Sylvia it would grow back longer. And one Christmas when I got a new baby doll that could open its mouth and say, 'Mama,' Catherine told me if it could open its mouth, it could eat sausages. It never said, 'Mama' again, and my beautiful doll Sylvia was destroyed.

Catherine was my protagonist, but she was also my protector, if anyone messed with me she would hunt them down and deal to them, she liked nothing more than to 'Kick Arse.'

Catherine took over as chief storyteller when Rosaleen left home. She told us the fascinating saga of Mrs. Shoe polish. She had an amazing imagination, and would make up all sorts of games for us to play.

We spent a lot of time in our bedroom. We always had to be in bed before Rosaleen, or John and Kevin could go out. When they left home we had to be in bed before dad could go to the pub.

It seemed someone was always wanting us to go to bed early so they could go out and have a life. We weren't entitled to one. It didn't matter if it was broad daylight and all the other kids were playing out in the street, we had to be in bed.

In the summer our beds would become swimming pools. We would roll the bedclothes down to the end to make an imaginary diving board, then we would dive into the middle of the bed and pretend to swim, racing to see who could reach the other end first. She always won. If she was ever in danger of losing a game she would change the rules to suit herself.

The games weren't always fun mind you. Catherine told me the wrinkles in the sheets at the bottom of my bed were snakes, and that they would wrap themselves around my legs when I was asleep. I would get so scared she would have to let me sleep in her bed. I still sleep with my knees under my chin. She told me so many ghost stories I was afraid of my own shadow.

She was always playing tricks on me. One night I got out of bed to go to the toilet. Our room was very dark as mum insisted on putting blackout curtains on the window. While I was out of the room Catherine got into my bed, crawled down to the bottom under the covers and lay in wait. I got back into bed, and just as I snuggled down, she grabbed both my ankles. I screamed, and screamed, and screamed, thinking the snakes had finally got me.

It wasn't all bad of course, she did save my life on more than one occasion.

Mum and dad took us to the beach one sunny, summer day. It was very hot and I wandered off to the sea with my inflatable lilo. I couldn't swim, so I draped myself across the lilo with my feet dangling in the water and paddled about. I was having a lovely time until I looked up and saw the beach had all but disappeared into the distance. I was caught in a rip. I tried not to panic and held on to the lilo all the time praying that it wouldn't burst. I could see the tiny ant-like people on the beach and recognised Catherine's bright green swimsuit. She was jumping up and down, pointing out to sea, pointing at me. A few minutes later a blue head came swimming towards me. The lifeguard grabbed the lilo and told me to hang on tight. I got safely back to shore expecting to be told off by mum and dad, but they weren't there. They didn't know I was in the water, and if it hadn't been for Catherine raising the alarm I might have made it to New Zealand a few years earlier, on a lilo.

Most nights we would go to bed hungry because we would have our dinner so early. Mum would have it ready for us before she went to work at four-thirty. It would be in the oven all dried up and disgusting.

When we got a bit older Catherine and I would scrape our dinner into the bin and just eat the chocolate biscuits mum brought home from the biscuit factory where she worked.

On the nights dad didn't go out to the pub we'd have to wait until he was settled in front of the telly, then we would creep downstairs. It was hard trying not to giggle, making sure we stepped over the creaky stairs. Going down the hallway was the most nerve-wracking, the kitchen was beside the living room, so we knew he could come out at any minute and catch us. Once safely in the kitchen we'd cut a slice of bread and smear it with tomato sauce. There was never much of anything else to eat in the house, no such thing as leftovers with six kids to feed.

Mum bought only what we needed every day at the corner shop. John and Kevin were always filled up with mountains of mashed potato every dinner time. We didn't have a fridge in the early days, but we did have a pantry that was as cold as the grave, jellies would set in there overnight.

So tomato sauce 'butty' in hand, we'd check the coast was clear, and make our way back down the hallway. All of a sudden the tension would become too much and we'd tear up the stairs as fast as we could, laughing and shrieking. Dad would come charging out of the living room like a wounded bull, "By Jesus, who's out of bed?" He would shout. But we'd already be in bed with our contraband safely hidden under the blankets. We knew he wouldn't bother coming up if we stayed quiet.

I remember on hot summer nights we'd get thirsty but we wouldn't be allowed a glass of water, so we'd go into the bathroom and suck the flannel. In our defence, we might have been too little to reach the tap.

I was woken up in the night many times as a small child by the sound of fighting coming from mum and dad's bedroom. I would lie awake listening, getting more and more frightened, terrified of where it would lead. Then a voice in the dark would say, "Ding Ding. Now in the blue corner we have dad, and in the red corner we have mum, Ding Ding, first-round goes to..." It was Catherine, she would turn their terrifying fighting into a boxing match and make me laugh. She was always the protector, always trying to fix things.

Our bedroom was on the second floor above the living room. When we walked around up there the light on the living room ceiling downstairs would swing back and forth. That was dad's signal we were out of bed.

One night I was lying in bed waiting for Catherine to get undressed, and get into bed. She was still wearing her school uniform and didn't seem in any hurry. She potted about, stomping around the room. I told her to hurry up so we wouldn't get into trouble, but she just ignored me. Meanwhile, the light on the living room ceiling started swinging. Dad shouted up. "Suzanne, get into bed." "It's not me," I said. Catherine carried on pottering about. Dad shouted up again. "Suzanne, get into bed." "It's not me," I said again.

I told Catherine to get a move on and get into bed before he came up, but she took no notice. Dad shouted up. "Suzanne, I won't tell you again. Get into bed!" "It's not me," I shouted. I was getting worried now. "Right, that's it, I'm coming up," he said.

Catherine dived into bed fully clothed, shoes and all, and pulled the blankets up under her chin. I didn't think that would save her, dad always ripped the covers off us when he was going to give us a hiding. He came pounding up the stairs, burst in the door, face like thunder, eyes blazing, and he came straight over to me. I started babbling, "It wasn't me. It wasn't me." He wasn't listening, he was in a blind rage. What made him look like he wanted to kill me just because he thought I was out of bed? He pulled my covers off and hit me so hard I'm sure I bounced a few feet off the bed. It was so unfair but I knew once he pulled Catherine's covers off he would know it wasn't me stomping around the room and feel sorry for hitting me. After he'd finished with me he turned around and left the room. I couldn't believe it, was there no justice in the world!

I lay there crying, feeling sorry for myself, then I heard Catherine's pathetic little voice saying. "Did it hurt?" "Yes, I think he broke my leg," I said. "Well, that's good then because if he has we can go to the police station and have him arrested." Cold comfort for me lying there with my leg throbbing with the pain.

Whenever we got a hiding Catherine would always ask me if it hurt. I thought it was because she felt sorry for me and wanted to make sure I was okay. But it was actually because she thought dad didn't hit me as hard as he hit her.

It was usually after one of these hidings we would start plotting to devise ways of killing Dad. Stabbing was the preferred option as knives were readily accessible. Also we didn't want it to be too quick, we wanted to look him in the eye so he would know it was us who did it, and we could say things to him like, "There, see how you like that then!" Seems hard to believe now, but it was very real at the time.

The thing that got us into the most trouble at night was our singing. We would sing for hours. 'Ten Green Bottles' could go on forever, and then there was our favourite, 'The Twelve Days of Christmas.' I can still hear it, 'Five Goooo-wooooo-ld Riiiiiiiiings…'

I will concede that we probably drove him mad with some of our antics. When we argued amongst ourselves we could spend hours trying to drown each other out by saying in our sing-song Scouse accents, "Listen to er, listen to er." Until someone shouted, "Shurrup or I'll bang your heads together."

As we got older we'd invent more interesting things to keep us occupied.

One of the challenges we set ourselves was to lean out of the window to try and touch the row of bricks jutting out from the wall below. Every night we'd take turns to see who would reach it first. We didn't seem to be getting any closer to our goal, so Catherine got very daring one night. She told me to hold her ankles so she could lean out a bit further than usual. So there she was hanging out of the window with her nightdress over her head, and I heard dad coming up the stairs. I was faced with a dilemma. Should I stay and hold onto her and take the risk we'd both get a hiding, or should I let go and save myself? It wasn't a hard decision. My survival instincts kicked in. I let go of her, jumped into bed, pulled the covers over my head, and pretended to be asleep.

It shows how frightened I was of him, I was prepared to let Catherine possibly fall to her death rather than face his wrath. Luckily she didn't fall. Dad hauled her back in, and gave her such a hiding. Needless to say I wasn't very popular after that, but I got paid back many times over the years.

It wasn't the only time Catherine was left dangling from a window. We went to a dance one night when we were teenagers. We came home drunk to find we'd been locked out. Catherine said her bedroom window was open so we crept around the back of the house trying not to disturb the dog, who barked his head off anyway, and probably woke the whole neighbourhood.

The window was very high up, so we collected all the outdoor tables and chairs and made them into a pyramid. "Up you go," I said. "Why me?" Said Catherine. "Because it's your window," I said, Irish logic coming to the fore once more.

She climbed up and managed to get her arms hooked over the windowsill just as the pyramid of outdoor furniture collapsed. I was helpless with laughter watching her dangling there. It was déjà vu!

I pulled myself together, climbed onto a chair, grabbed her feet and pushed. She sailed over the window sill, across the bed, and landed with a heap on the floor at mum's feet. She looked up at mum standing there angry with her arms crossed and said. "For God's sake, if you were awake, why didn't you let us in!"

Catherine got a two-wheeler bike when she was nine. I know! The unfairness of it all! To her credit, she was good at sharing. We went everywhere together on that bike. Me on the pedals doing all the work, and her sitting on the seat like lady muck, giving directions.

One evening I was peddling hell for leather around a corner on the wrong side of the road, the next thing I knew I was laying on my back on someone's front lawn, and Catherine was embedded in the hedge. We'd crashed into a car coming the other way. The driver came over to see if we were alright, he wanted to take us home and speak to our parents.

That's the last thing we wanted, we were supposed to be in bed, mum and dad were both out and we'd left our little sister Jayne alone in the house.

The next accident we were in together was a little more serious. I was fifteen and the car we were passengers in drove into the back of a stationary vehicle. I was knocked unconscious and came too with Catherine dragging me out of the car screaming, "There's petrol leaking, it's gonna blow!" It was just water from the cracked radiator, but she likes a drama. Anyway it was nice of her to try and save my life again. By the time we got back to our house she was hysterical and the accident had grown out of all proportion. Dad was most concerned and plied her with whiskey to calm her down, it took most of the night. Meanwhile, I sat quietly on the couch with a broken wrist, hoping someone was going to notice and take me to the hospital. They didn't. I took myself off to the doctor the next day. He was most disgusted that I'd been left in so much pain all night.

When I was eleven Catherine insisted I shave my legs, she said it was either that, or join the circus. I reluctantly went into the bathroom and got dad's razor. It was a brutal experience. It was razor-sharp and kept twirling around, by the time I'd finished there was blood everywhere, Sweeney Todd couldn't have made more of a mess. Dad knew someone had used his razor, but he never guessed it was me, I was too young.

Catherine had to help me clean the bathroom so I wouldn't say it had been her idea.

I was thirteen when she insisted I pluck my eyebrows. She said I could give Groucho Marx a run for his money. We went off to the chemist, bought some tweezers and plucked my eyebrows into oblivion. They never grew back.

For years Catherine and I would race each other home from school every lunch hour. We didn't like using the school toilets, they were outside in the freezing cold and never had any toilet paper, so it was always a mad dash to see who could get in there first when we got home. She always won.

We were reminiscing about our silly competitions many years later, and we were laughing so much we both needed to go to the toilet. We looked at each other, both having the same idea, and took off down the hall to the toilet. Catherine got their first as usual and slammed the door in my face. I hammered on the door. "Get lost!" she said. I could hear her laughing so I hammered on the door again. "Get lost you!" she said again, she was getting annoyed. I saw mum coming down the hallway so I hammered on the door once more, gave it a kick, and ran off into the bedroom. Mum came along and innocently knocked on the toilet door to see if it was free. Catherine yelled out, "Piss of you, ye bitch!" thinking it was me. Mums face was a picture. "Well, that's very nice I must say!" she said.

I had many interested, exciting, and dangerous adventures growing up with Catherine. When I look back on it now I see being banished to the bedroom all those years made us use our imagination. We wouldn't have so many funny memories if we had sat in front of a TV every night. We weren't allowed any toys to play with, or books to read, but we still had a lot of fun. It was usually the fun that got us into trouble, but there was always 'laughter with the tears.

Things changed once we left England. Catherine was sixteen and she seemed to grow up overnight. She got a job and a boyfriend, and for the first time in our lives we slept in separate bedrooms. It felt as though I'd lost my ally, my singing partner, and my partner in crime.

Mischief

Full of 'mitchery,' up to no good,

we would behave if we could.

But we were trapped in our room with nothing to do

no toys, no books, just us two.

Imagination was the key,

to a whole new world of fantasy.

A secret life both of us shared,

nobody knew, nobody cared.

As long as we stayed in our room, in our beds,

and didn't disturb with the singing dad dreads,

we could be anyone, we could go anywhere,

forget for a while we were trapped up there.

JAYNE

I was jealous of Jayne for so many reasons known only to a sibling full of rivalry. I can still see her all wrapped up warm in her pram on the front doorstep, while I was outside exposed to the elements, freezing.

When mum took us to the shops I would have to run alongside the pram hanging on to the cold metal handle trying to keep up, thinking all the while, that pram used to be mine, while Jayne got a nice warm comfortable ride.

I was always sick with colds as a child and I was warned not to go near the new baby in-case she caught my germs. So I did the only thing I could do armed with that information, I hung over her cot every chance I got and breathed on her. She didn't die though, and I have to admit I was relieved, being brought up a Catholic you quickly learn you could potentially burn in hell for all eternity if your sin is big enough. Killing your sister is definitely a mortal sin.

Jayne was outgoing and friendly. When she was little she would swing on the front gate waiting for people to walk by so she could talk to them. Sometimes she would go off with them and disappear. Some boys took her away one day and didn't bring her back, mum had to send out a search party. Jayne was eventually found miles away from home wandering around by herself, lost.

It's a wonder she survived her childhood we didn't look after her very well. What with John terrorising her, leaving her on buses and letting her wander off with strangers, not to mention dropping a wardrobe on top of her. Well we won't mention that…

We found her just in time one day. She was balanced on a chair with her head buried in the medicine cabinet at the top of the Welsh dresser in the kitchen, stuffing dad's 'Smarties' into her mouth. Even though they looked like Smarties, and dad had told us that's what they were, Catherine and I were old enough to know they were actually his heart pills. Jayne didn't come to any harm but Catherine and I got the blame for not keeping an eye on her. Dad got away with being so irresponsible.

Jayne and I were never close and fought most of the time. It was dad who gave us our first special moment together when we went to see him at the funeral home. She'd brought him his shillelagh to help him on his journey, he always liked a walking stick.

All I could think of while we where there was that this was our last chance to get a DNA sample to prove once and for all if he was Catherine's father.

When we saw dad Jayne started to cry, and for the first time in my life I put my arm around her as a sister and we cried together.

My Shillelagh

Think of me when you come across a twisted piece of wood.

Lying there upon the ground in a place where I once stood.

8. OUR HOUSE

I was two and a half when we moved into our first proper house in Liverpool. The first few years of my life had been spent crammed into a flat with four siblings on the second floor of the block of flats where I was born. Mum was desperate to get out of the flats, especially after I went head first down the two flights of concrete steps at just eighteen months old. She sent one of the older kids down to check on me, she couldn't bear to look, she thought I was dead for sure. She'd built a gate at the top of the stairs, but we shared the landing with another family, there were so many kids coming and going, the gate was always left open.

Mum and dad weren't English, they were told they had to have lived in England for five years before they could even put their name on the housing list. The war had been over for fifteen years, but Liverpool had been a prime target and was devastated by the bombings so housing was still scarce.

I remember going into town on the bus when I was small and seeing all the bombed-out houses. I was fascinated to see the inside of one house with its pink wallpaper, and the sink still attached to the upstairs bathroom wall.

Mum and dad's name finally came up on the housing list after ten years of waiting and they were given a corporation house to rent. Not a moment too soon as it turned out, there was another baby on the way.

Our new house was two-story, semi-detached, with three bedrooms and a garden. Mum said was in a bit of a state, but it was far cry from where we had been living.

The day we moved into our new house has stayed in my memory, even though I was so young. My brothers and sisters were running through the empty rooms, excitement boiling over at having so much space after living in a small flat for all those years. They ran upstairs to check out their new bedrooms, I toddled along as fast as I could.

By the time I got to the top of the stairs, they had all disappeared. I looked in all the rooms but there was no sign of them. In the biggest room, I saw a cupboard on the wall, the door was open slightly. I went over and peeped inside. They all jumped out at me yelling "Surprise!" I got the biggest fright and I cried and cried. They had to quickly calm me down, I was the baby, no-one was allowed to upset me.

The house was in a predominately Catholic neighbourhood and on Sunday mornings when the church bells rang out people would come out of their houses all heading in the same direction towards the church. There was standing room only at every mass. Most of the kids in the area went to the Catholic school attached to the church so we all knew each other, it was a real community.

You could always tell who the Catholics were when a funeral procession went down the main road. They'd all stop dead in their tracks, bow their heads and make the sign of the cross.

Apart from going to Mass every Sunday, our religion didn't play a big part in our home life. The only real concession we made to being Catholics was eating fish on Fridays. Mum would boil some kind of disgusting fish with milk, the smell was terrible. It was a big meaty sort of fish, we could have had sword fights with the bones they were so big. We had to dissect the fish into tiny pieces on our plate to make it safe to eat. It was stressful, you just never knew if that meal would be your last supper.

Our new house was cold. Mum would put masking tape around the windows to keep out the draughts. In the winter we'd leave our clothes at the end of our beds so we could pull them under the covers and get dressed in the bed. We didn't have carpet on the floor in the bedroom just cold vinyl.

I got very good at jumping from my bed, through the doorway, onto the strip of carpet on the landing outside. Making the return trip wasn't so easy. One night I took a flying leap, landed on the bed and all the legs shot out from under it, me and the bed went crashing to the floor.

There were old fashioned gas fires on the walls in two of the bedrooms but we weren't allowed to use them, mum said they weren't safe, but I think she was just worried we would catch fire. We'd found an old bible in the loft when we first moved into the house. Inside were newspaper clippings about a family who had lived in the house before us. A ten-year-old girl burned to death in mums bedroom when her nightdress had caught fire. Luckily Mum never found out about our little storytelling adventure gathered around the gas fire in the bedroom with Rosaleen.

We ate all our meals in the kitchen. Sunday lunch was the only meal dad shared with us. He didn't allow any talking at the table while we were eating, he said he didn't like having his dinner rammed down his throat. Of course when you're a kid and you're told not to make a sound, you just have to kick someone under the table to try and get them into trouble. Then they would just have to kick you back, and then you would start giggling, so your plan would backfire and you'd be the one sent out of the room. It doesn't sound like much of a punishment, but it was freezing in the hallway.

There was a clothes rack above the kitchen table on a pulley. It's not pleasant having wet washing dripping down the back of your neck when you're eating, but it was a necessity. It was hopeless trying to get the washing dry outside, it was always raining. On the odd occasion the washing could be hung outside, it would come in dirtier than when it went out because of the coal smut coming from all the chimneys. Mum did all the washing by hand in the kitchen sink for many years.

The old Welsh dresser was against one wall, it held everything from cups and saucers to dads 'Smarties', and mum's red lipstick.

Alongside that was a sideboard full of ironing, a few miscellaneous items, and the money box. When I went to grammar school mum put money in the money box every week for my school fees, lunches, and bus fare. She never locked it which was a bit naïve, but I only ever stole enough to buy extra lunch, I was always hungry.

The kitchen was the warmest room in the house. I looked forward to going down to breakfast every morning to thaw out beside the old paraffin heater. The fumes from the heater filled the air, and probably poisoned it too. I always had chest problems when I was a kid. Mum blamed the fog, not the heater. She'd send me across the road on a message to the 'chandlers' store every week to fill up the paraffin container. The paraffin wasn't just used for heating.

Head-lice were a constant problem, and mum's solution was to douse our heads in paraffin. She would give us a flannel to hold over our eyes to hopefully prevent blindness, then we would bend over the sink while she poured the paraffin over our heads. It would sting so badly, but if you opened your mouth to cry you'd get a lungful of toxic fumes.

Grounds for child abuse... I should say so!

Paraffin is waterproof, so for weeks afterwards we wouldn't be able to get soap to lather up when our hair was washed. Nevertheless, we had the shiniest hair around, everyone asked us what shampoo we used. How could we tell them it was 'Stardrops' liquid detergent. 'Makes your floors shine and your dishes sparkle.'

The 'Chandlers' shop where I got the paraffin was an Alladins Cave, they sold everything from brooms to pots and pans, to mousetraps. I went in there one day and saw the most beautiful coffee tables I had ever seen. They were typical sixties with tapered legs and little gold feet, and they had a glass top. But best of all, underneath the glass was a picture of the Beatles. There was Ringo's lovely face smiling up at me. As soon as I saw it I thought, "God! We have to have one of those." I ran home and told Catherine to come back with me and have a look. As soon as she saw Paul McCartney's lovely face smiling up at her she said, "God! We have to have one of those."

We went home and told mum all about the coffee tables and begged and pleaded for her to buy one. She said she'd think about it. When we got home from school the next day she told us to go and look in the living room. We couldn't get there fast enough. Sure enough, there was the coffee table sitting in the middle of the floor. We ran over to get our first glimpse of the Beatles in our house. But the picture was of ballerinas, she hadn't bought the Beatles one. So disappointing!

I thought she liked the Beatles. After all, she'd taken us to the pictures in Liverpool to see their movie 'A Hard Day's Night' a few years earlier when it was first released. It was a frightening experience for a four-year-old. As soon as the curtains drew back the whole theatre erupted, everyone was screaming and jumping up and down. I thought there must be a fire and looked over at mum expecting to get the signal to run for my life. I didn't hear a word of the movie, the screaming never stopped. I was glad when it was over and we could get out of there.

Apart from a new coffee table with 'ballerinas,' there was also a coal fire in the living room in the early days. This was eventually replaced by a gas heater. It was a shame, the open fire was good for making toast and roasting chestnuts. Catherine and I roasted some chestnuts one night when everyone was out. We lined them up along the front of the fire, sat down to watch telly, and forgot all about them.

We had to dive for cover behind the couch when hot molten fireballs started exploding all around the room, leaving little scorch marks on the wallpaper.

We missed the coal fire when it went, but we didn't miss going out to the coal shed to fill up the bucket every night in the dark.

On Saturday's the whole family would gather in the living room to watch the matinee movie on the telly. It was one of the few things we did together as a family. Even dad would be there sometimes, although he was usually asleep in the chair, sleeping off his last drinking bout, and getting ready for his next. He did love cowboy films though. He would watch, totally engrossed right through to the end, then get up and say, "Load of Yankee bull!" every single time!

Mum always kept a packet of toffees hidden in the kitchen cupboard, but we could never ask for them. We had to wait until she gave the signal, then we'd all get jammed in the doorway trying to get to them first. Watching telly was really bad for your teeth. The wind and rain would be battering the windows, the fire would be roaring in the grate, and mum's knitting needles would be clacking away twenty to the dozen churning out another fashion disaster.

While we were all watching telly together one day, we decided to join in with John's interesting pastime. John was a nervous child, and had a habit of rocking back and forth.

It was probably a sign of severe emotional disturbance, but we just thought it looked like fun. We were all lined up on the couch, John, Catherine, me and Jayne, all rocking back and forth in unison bouncing off the back of the couch. All of a sudden we heard this massive 'rip,' then, 'twang,' 'boing,' 'ping.' All the springs burst out of the back of the couch. We waited in horror to see what mum would say. She just laughed, the thought of being able to buy a new one outweighing her annoyance. There was no more rocking once the new lounge suite arrived. John had to make do with chewing his fingernails.

Our house was always in a state of re-decoration. We were constantly moving from room to room while the next one was wallpapered and painted. Mum and dad would start at one end of the house and by the time they'd reached the other end it was time to start again. It was a nightmare, and it didn't just interfere with our living arrangements.

Every Monday morning there was a uniform inspection at my high school. My shoes were falling apart so I was singled out every week and given a note to take home to my parents asking them to buy me new shoes. I gave the notes to mum but all she said was, "I can't afford new shoes, I've just had to buy wallpaper and paint. Do they think we're made of money?"

After a couple of weeks of this it was getting embarrassing, so the next time I was pulled up I told the nuns I couldn't have new shoes because we didn't have any money. The look of sympathy on the nun's face was quickly replaced by a look of remorse when she remembered how she'd humiliated me every week. I wonder if she would have been so sympathetic if she'd known we had the best looking house in the street.

The DIY madness didn't just stop at decoration. I woke up one morning to an incredible banging coming from downstairs. I went down and found mum with a sledgehammer in her hand, knocking down the brick wall between the hallway and the parlour. I was alarmed to say the least. Had mum finally cracked under the strain of having six kids and an alcoholic husband? I knew for a fact I wouldn't be visiting her if she got taken away and locked up. I'd been to one of those places, and had no desire to go back.

I was eleven at the time and had signed up for a club at school. It was all about volunteering to go out into the community to help people. I thought it would be a good way to make friends. I met up with another girl from the club outside school one Saturday afternoon for my first assignment. No-one had told me we had to do this in our spare time, I was hoping to get time off school for doing good deeds. I should have known then that I wasn't cut out for that self-sacrificing lark.

The girl wouldn't tell me where we were going, if she had I would never have gone. We arrived outside a huge, ugly, dark Victorian building. There were big iron gates at the front with enormous padlocks on them. I looked around with trepidation and saw the sign: 'Mental Institution.' My insides turned to liquid, and I would have run away if my legs hadn't turned to jelly. We rang the bell on the gate and a nun came to let us in. She led us through freezing cold long corridors. I kept my eyes pointing to the floor, I didn't want to see anything disturbing that would haunt me forever. All I can remember seeing is a room full of women, all wearing the same shapeless floral dresses, and all with their heads shaved. It was a shocking sight.

Oh, the nightmares I had after that visit. In my dream I would follow the nun out to the main gate, counting the steps until I would be free from that horrible place. Then just as we'd get to the gate she would turn to me and say, "Sorry, but you can't leave."

Anyway, the answer to why mum was knocking the wall down wasn't quite so disturbing. 'Open plan living.' That's what she had in mind. I think she might even have invented the term.

She didn't stop with the hallway, she knocked the wall through to the pantry and coal shed to extend the kitchen. Sounds lovely but all this DIY wasn't good for happy family relations. Not that we knew what they were anway.

The arguing and fighting escalated to new levels when the paintbrushes came out and it left me with an irrational fear of wallpaper.

The dynamics of the house changed over the years. It started out with eight of us crammed in for about four years, but I was only six when the older kids started to leave home. The way they left home one by one reminds me of a song Catherine and I used to sing on one of our many singing soirées while we were banished to the bedroom.

There were six in the bed, and the little one said, "Roll over, roll over."

So they all rolled over and one fell out, there were five in the bed, and the little one said, "Roll over, roll over …"

We didn't all sleep in the same bed of course, but as each one left, there was more room for the rest of us to spread out.

Laughter With The Tears

The Two Storey Semi

The two-story semi was home too so many,
how did we fit, when we all lived in it.

Four girls all sharing, but never past caring
for their privacy and space, it was always the case.

Two boys had their privacy, their own little dynasty
free from the rabble, and female babble.

Mum and dad across the landing,
close enough for handing,
out punishment and smacks, for any wisecracks.

It was comfortable and cozy, even for Posy
the first one to leave, and let us all breathe.

Move on and spread, out that's what it's about.
More room to please, less need to tease,
one another about their failings no doubt.

Soon only three, were left with the key
to the two-story semi, that was home too so many.

9. DING-DING

I'd like to know what made dad fly into such rages. It usually happened when he was sober. Maybe he needed a drink and didn't have any money. Maybe he'd seen a different future for himself and we came along and spoiled it.

From the outside our family looked the same as everyone else's, but we had a secret. The secret was never talked about, not even amongst ourselves, it was just something we lived with on a daily basis. We didn't know that violence wasn't normal family behaviour.

Dad was always threatening us. "I'll break both your legs" he'd say. " I'll throw you through that wall." Or, "If I get my hands on you, you won't stand up for a week." And my least favourite one, "I'll break your back for ya." Like he was doing us a favour! It sounds quite terrifying, and we were certainly scared, but he never followed through with any of those terrible threats. We just got the odd hiding and were constantly being picked on and ground down.

Years after I'd left home mum told me she was always glad when dad was picking on one of us because it meant he left her alone.

The one person in the world who could have protected us was just glad it wasn't happening to her!

Violence was around us all the time but we managed to live with it, and get through it, kids are quite resilient. But when they are exposed to things they shouldn't see it puts an old head on young shoulders, it stunts their growth emotionally and makes them insecure.

A Punch and Judy show came to our school when I was about five. All the kids were sitting on the floor in the main hall waiting excitedly. The little stage was in front of us all bright stripey colours with little blue velvet curtains. The curtains were pulled back, and we all cheered when the show started. Punch hit his wife Judy, then Judy hit Punch over the head with a stick, then the policeman came. All the kids were laughing, I couldn't see what was so funny, didn't they have a family like mine?

My older brothers and sisters had big responsibilities. From a young age, they had a lot to deal with, they were the ones at the front line. I was lucky, most of the time I could just fade into the shadows and wait until the fighting was over.

It was especially hard for my brothers. They would try and stand up to dad but it was hard when they were just boys. I don't know what that did to them knowing they couldn't protect their mum.

Rosaleen had the hardest time, it was her job to try and put a stop to the fighting, she was the only one who could calm dad down, he listened to her.

When I was very young she came into our bedroom one night, plonked down on my bed, put her head in her hands and burst into tears. We asked her why she was crying and she said, "You'd cry too if you'd just seen the way he hit her." It wasn't the sort of thing two little girls wants to hear, but we were the only ones she could share it with, no-one else could know.

I don't remember if there were any bruises to be seen, but I do remember mum's friend Mrs. Jones coming round for her weekly cup of tea and a chat. She must have noticed something because when mum left the room for a few minutes she started quizzing me about my dad and what went on in our house. I didn't tell of course, kids never do.

One night we were woken up by a commotion outside our bedroom. We heard Kevin being told to go downstairs and ring the police. After a while when Kevin didn't come back up Catherine and I were sent down to see what was happening. Kevin was fast asleep on the telephone, he hadn't called them. He got a clip around the ear hole for that. The policeman eventually came, he was very young, I don't know who looked more embarrassed, him or my dad. Dad did his usual grovelling, 'Yes officer, no officer,' trying to convince him what a fine upstanding citizen he was.

The policeman just told him to behave himself in future and left. We thought he would take dad away to the police station, but domestic violence was considered a private affair in those days, not a police matter. We were scared what dad would do to us after the policeman left, but he just went back to bed. He'd learned his lesson, for a little while at least.

The violence didn't just affect our lives. Dad was never one for close friends but he did have one in his younger days. I don't know how they met, but it was probably in the pub, dad never went anywhere else.

Jimmy lived with his elderly mother, he'd never married or had any children. He was a gentle giant and we all loved him. He spent a lot of time at our house, we were his surrogate family. He never seemed to mind us bothering him, and I would fight my sisters' for a place on his lap every time he sat down. I secretly wished he was my real dad. It was good having him there when 'the drink' reared its ugly head. He would do his best to calm the situation down and protect my mum. We felt safe with him around.

One afternoon after a drinking session thing's turned ugly yet again. The trouble was escalating, so mum ran to get away from dad. He went after her, he hadn't finished what he'd started. Jimmy and our Kevin, who was only fifteen at the time, tried to intervene. In the ensuing scuffle Jimmy fell, landing across the rigid arm of dad's chair. It looked as though he might have broken a few ribs, he was in a lot of pain.

Dad was very apologetic and of course, blamed 'the drink.' Jimmy wouldn't go to the hospital because he needed to get home to his bedridden mother. Mum bound his ribs to make it easier for him to get around. Not the best thing to do, but that's what they did in those days.

About a week later Jimmy came round to our house and asked mum what it meant if he was coughing up blood. Mum and dad took him to the hospital straight away. They sat in the waiting room while Jimmy was being examined, he was in there a long time. The doctor eventually came out and told mum and dad to go in and say goodbye to Jimmy as he didn't have long to live. They couldn't believe what they were hearing. "But he's only got broken ribs," Dad said. The doctor told them Jimmy had pneumonia brought on by the broken ribs and that he was also in the final stages of tuberculosis. His lungs had wasted away.

I don't remember being told Jimmy had died, and I never got to go to the funeral, I was only seven. The following week we all had to go to the clinic to get immunised against tuberculosis as it can be contagious.

There was an inquest into Jimmy's death. Mum testified he was drinking whiskey at the time of the accident, which was true. The coroner concluded that he fell because he'd had too much to drink, which of course wasn't true.

I know it was an accident, and I know he would have died soon anyway, but I can't help thinking we invited him into our family and we killed him.

Sometimes

Sometimes there was fighting

Sometimes there were tears

Sometimes there was silence

Hiding all my fears

Sometimes there was shouting

Sometimes it was still

Sometimes I was frightened

But I knew the drill

Sometimes I felt lonely

Sometimes I was scared

Sometimes I was left to doubt

If anybody cared

Sometimes now I'm older

Sometimes when I recall

Sometimes I wish I could erase

The memory of it all

I'd like to say that was a turning point and 'the drink' took a back seat from then on, but nothing changed. If anything the guilt made dad drink more.

Even when he went into the rest-home he still managed to go for a drink most days. The week before he died he polished off a bottle of whiskey, and even though he was on oxygen and could hardly breathe, he still managed to get to the pub. 'The drink' won in the end, it always did!

Just before we moved to New Zealand there was another huge fight. I don't remember what it was about, or how it started, I don't suppose it matters, most of these fights had the same theme. Dad would come home drunk, mum would confront him, then he would start accusing her of having affairs and things would get out of hand.

Things went too far this one time, and somehow mum ended up with a broken finger. Rosaleen was living with us at the time and when she came home from work and saw what happened she packed us all up and we left the house. We stayed away for the whole day to let dad stew. While we were away we had a big long talk to mum trying to persuade her it was time to leave him. We told her things were never going to get any better, he was never going to change. Rosaleen said she had her own family to take care of now and she wasn't always going to be around to pick up the pieces anymore. We tried to persuade mum that she didn't have to stay with him, we would all support her.

We didn't even have to take him to New Zealand with us, he didn't want to go anyway, why not leave him behind? She seemed to agree.

We went back to the house in the evening. Dad was sitting in the middle of the lounge on one of our remaining chairs, all the other ones had been sold ready for the move. He was feeling sorry for himself as usual, he hated to be ignored. Mum went to talk to him in the living room and tell him she was leaving while the rest of us went upstairs to the bedroom to wait.

We waited and waited, sick with worry, not knowing what was going to happen. Was this it, was she finally going to leave him and give us a peaceful life? It was hard to imagine what it would be like.

Mum was gone so long we started to get worried. We weren't sure what he would do to her when she told him she was leaving, he'd always threatened to kill her, or burn the house down if she left. We were scared for ourselves too, we knew he'd blame us for talking her into it.

We couldn't stand the suspense any longer, so Rosaleen sent Catherine and I downstairs to check what was happening. Catherine looked through the keyhole. "Oh God no!" she said. "What is it?" I cried, imagining the worst. She moved out of the way to let me look. I couldn't believe my eyes, mum was sitting on dad's knee laughing. The relief and the disappointment had a race to the finish line inside my head.

We'd been through all that stress and upheaval for nothing. Was it just a game to them?

I only remember Mum fighting back once. It was the year before we left England and dad had become even more unbearable to live with. We'd already had to call the police once, but by the time they'd arrived, dad had run up the stairs and jumped into bed. He was sitting there all sweetness and light and said, "Good evening Constable, what can I do for you?" Dad was terrified of the police, but he did concede that in certain circumstances they were a necessary evil.

Tensions were already running high, but when Dad came home from the pub one afternoon 'waltzing drunk,' they boiled over. Dad went too far this time, he accused mum of having an affair with his old friend Jimmy. Of all the terrible things he could have said, that was the worst. Mum was sitting on the couch peeling an apple with a small knife. She jumped up, lunged over to him and put the knife to his throat. I'd never seen her so angry. She was yelling at him, "You take that back, go on take it back." Dad was scared. I stood and watched, and all I could think was, finally! Do it, just do it, finish him off and put us out of our misery once and for all.

Every argument culminated in dad accusing mum of having an affair, he was a very possessive and jealous man, she had to account for her whereabouts at all times.

If she was on the phone for more than a few minutes he would go mad, even if it was one of us kids ringing. "You'll end up with a cauliflower ear," he'd say.

When mum got her computer he felt even more threatened. He sidled up to me one day and just by the way, asked me how much electricity the computer used. He was hoping they used a lot of electricity so he would have an excuse to complain about the power bill. I didn't know, but I knew what he was up to, so I said, "Oh, about as much as a light bulb." His disappointment was evident, now he'd have to think of something else.

His main obsession stemmed from the time of their separation before Catherine was born. They'd had a particularly nasty fight and dad said he was going to kill her when he came home from work the next day. Mum went into work black and blue, picked up her cards, and caught the train to London. She saved herself, but at what cost to the children.

Even though Rosaleen was only nine she had to take over and look after John and Kevin. Dad went to pieces and tried to kill himself with an overdose. He couldn't cope with the kids and was planning to put them into care before his sister, Aunty Betty, stepped in and took them. She already had half a dozen kids of her own, so it was a terrible situation.

Kevin stopped talking, they thought he'd gone deaf. They were going to take him to the hospital, but it was just the trauma of losing his mum so abruptly with no explanation, a hard thing for a five-year-old to comprehend.

John remembers running down the street hanging onto her skirt begging her not to go and being told to go home. He suffered his own trauma while she was away when Aunty Betty's husband hung him out of a three-story window by his ankles for wetting the bed. Rosaleen also suffered at the hands of her uncle.

Mum came home three months later after deciding she couldn't live without the kids. She just turned up on the doorstep one day with a policeman for protection. Kevin answered the door, took one look at her and ran away.

Dad should never have taken her back because he never forgave her. Every time they fought he would accuse her of running off with another man and only coming back because she was pregnant.

Mum got pregnant very soon after she got home, so dad never believed Catherine was his child. Mum was so relieved when I was born because we looked so much alike, she thought that would prove to him that Catherine was his.

During these fights, we would all jump to mums defence and tell him to stop saying such terrible things. Mum always denied the accusations and we believed her. It wasn't until she was in her seventies that she finally told us the truth. There had been another man. She'd met him at work. When she came into work that morning and said she was leaving for London, he went with her. They moved into a flat together and she got a job at a department store. When she decided she needed to go home for the kids he offered to marry her and take them all to live in South Africa. Whatever her reasons, mum said no, and told the man not to contact her again. So! Dad was right after all, he usually was.

They split up once more when they were in their late sixties. We were all getting on with our own lives at the time and didn't know what to make of it, or what to do about it. We ended up taking sides and it split the whole family down the middle. Once again dad tried to kill himself, and Rosaleen was left to deal with it.

When they decided they'd been apart long enough, they got back together, leaving the rest of us with a lot of bridge mending to do with each other. You'd think we would have known better than to get mixed up in their silly games after all those years, but we could never walk away and leave them without worrying.

Even though the violence slowed down over the years, it never really stopped. Dad was in his seventies when he broke his toe trying to kick the bedroom door down when mum had barricaded herself in. Once again Rosaleen was called on to help, but she was hundreds of kilometres away and couldn't do anything except worry. Rosaleen has had to deal with their marriage all her life. They should have called me. I would have phoned the police and got them to send the armed offenders out. That would have scared the bejesus out of him and put an end to his shenanigans once and for all.

The biggest regret of my childhood was not helping mum when she needed me. She came into my room one night and asked if she could get into my bed. I was all warm and cozy and didn't want to be disturbed so I said, "No go away, there's no room."

She went across to Catherine's bed and asked if she could get in with her. Catherine just pulled her covers back without hesitation, and mum got in. My first reaction was jealousy, I didn't want her in my sister's bed. Then came the guilt, I should have let her get in with me. I didn't know it then but she was just looking for a safe place to sleep after yet another fight with my dad. I was very young, only about three, but I never forgot that night.

I was finally able to make amends over forty years later. Mum needed a safe secure place to live when she finally left dad after fifty-nine years. I bought her a house around the corner from me. Just my way of saying, "Yes, you can get into my bed."

Young children feel things deeply, they blame themselves for things that were never their fault. They can spend a lifetime trying to understand what it was all about, and why it had to be that way.

Mum

What do you want mum why did you wake me,
I don't understand am not able to see.

There's no room for you here, it's not safe for you there,
but I didn't know I was too young to care.

The danger you faced, you had no-where to go,
no-one to turn to, no-one could know.

You'd made your bed, said your wedding vows,
what liberties that allows.

You looked for a haven, a safe place to stay,
with your three-year-old daughter who sent you away.

As the years went by I began to see,
and to understand what you needed from me.

The shame and the guilt settled into my heart,
all through my life it played a big part.

Until finally one day I was able to say,
put your trust in me mum I will make it okay.

You'll be safe and secure for the rest of your life,
something not found when you were a wife.

10. BEING IRISH

I thought dad drank because he was Irish, that he was born that way and didn't have a choice. To me drinking and being Irish went hand in hand. I was determined there would be no alcoholic Irish blood running through my veins.

When dad first moved to England just after the war there were only certain pubs he was allowed into, some of them had signs in the windows saying, 'No Dogs, No Irish.' The Irish were always unpopular in England, but probably never more so than when I was growing up.

The troubles in Ireland were spilling over onto English soil and were starting to have an impact on our daily lives culminating with the bombings in the seventies. Everywhere we went we would be evacuated because of a bomb scare. We never knew if it was for real, but it always had to be taken seriously.

I never felt Irish. I couldn't deny my heritage, but I didn't want any part of it. I never told anyone my Dad was Irish. It was a difficult time for me, but I can only imagine how tough his life became during that time, with his Irish accent.

I was about eight years old when I was first made aware of what was happening in the world around me. I met my friend on the way to school one morning and she was crying. I asked her what was wrong and she said, "The Irish have killed my brother."

Well that's just typical I thought. I asked her why the Irish had killed her brother and she told me he was a soldier in the British Army serving in Northern Ireland. I didn't know what any of that meant, but I thought about my two older brothers and knew I'd cry too if the Irish killed them. Well maybe not Kevin…

About five years later I was sitting in school one afternoon quietly dozing through my English class when the fire alarms went off. I just thought it was a drill they'd forgotten to tell us about, so I carried on snoozing. After a few minutes I could hear a lot of commotion in the corridor and started to feel a bit uneasy. Looking around the room I could see the other girls were getting worried too. The teacher seemed oblivious to the panic rising in her classroom. Finally one of the girls said, "Excuse me miss, I think that was the fire alarm." The teacher went outside to investigate and came back looking pale.

She said, "Right girls, that was the fire alarm. You know the drill, leave everything at your desks and file quickly and quietly out of the classroom, there's been a phone call to say that there is a bomb in the school."

Drill, what drill? We all ran screaming for the door, all knowledge of the correct procedure was forgotten, it was every girl for herself. Luckily I was on the ground floor, the school was five stories high, I wouldn't have wanted to be in the stairwells with seven hundred terrified girls all trying to get down at once.

We were told to line up outside in the playground which I thought was ridiculous, the whole school was made of glass, we weren't far enough away, if a bomb had gone off we would have all been killed. I thought we should have gone into the field and got down behind the fence, but what did I know!

While the teachers came around taking the roll the headmistress, an elderly nun, collapsed. In the ensuing panic all thoughts of the bomb were forgotten and we were told to go back into the school, get our things and go home. My coat was in the cloakroom but there was no way I was going back into the school, risking my life for the sake of a coat. But then I imagined the look on my mum's face if I came home without it. All hesitation was gone, I ran as fast as I could through the corridors praying all the way. It was terrifying not knowing if I was going to make it out alive.

I got home from school and burst in the back door. Mum was at the kitchen sink peeling potatoes as always. "What are you doing home so early?" She said.

"Guess what!" I said, hardly able to contain myself. "We had a bomb scare at school and the headmistress collapsed in front of us and got taken away in an ambulance and I think she's dead." "Well, take those shoes off and go put your slippers on." She said.

We were told at school the next day that the headmistress had died on the way to the hospital. The priest came and said mass for her at school, everyone was crying. Afterward we were told to go back to class and get on with our school work. No counselling in those days, we were tough, it was never talked about again. I was worried, what if they found out my dad was Irish and thought I had something to do with it?

Of course it wasn't the Irish that made the phone call, it was just a stupid prank, one that backfired. I felt sure the story would be front-page news. I searched the Liverpool Echo only to find a tiny article at the bottom of page eleven. It was just a small story in a time of much bigger ones.

Many years later my husband came home from work one day and told me there had been a bomb scare at the army barracks. He was a soldier, working in bomb disposal believe it or not, life can be stranger than fiction. Something inside of me came boiling to the surface. I rang the local radio station to give everyone a piece of my mind. "Didn't they know how dangerous it was playing stupid pranks like that? Didn't they know people could die? Didn't they know how traumatised people get?"

I guess I wasn't so tough after all, and could have used some counselling back then, when I was thirteen.

My opinion of the Irish eventually changed when I was given a book about the 'potato famine.' I didn't want to read it, I had no sympathy for people who thought they could survive solely on potatoes. What did they expect would happen when the potato crops failed? Why couldn't they grow carrots or some other vegetable for God's sake! I was completely ignorant of my own history.

I decided to read the book, but with a closed mind. It was a good story, and I was soon engrossed. It was a heart-rending tale of love and loss, starvation and corruption.

About halfway through the book it suddenly dawned on me, these were my people I was reading about, my ancestors that were being starved to death because of other people's greed. My great grandparents lived through that terrible time, if they hadn't survived, I wouldn't be here today. I cried my way through to the end of the book. I finally accepted there was Irish blood running through my veins, Non-alcoholic though.

11. IRELAND

We went to Ireland for our summer holidays two years in a row when I was six and seven. The memory of those trips have merged into one and the only thing that separates them in my memory is that on our first trip John and Kevin came with us and my Granddad was still alive. On the second trip John and Kevin stayed home and Granddad wasn't there, he'd died earlier in the year.

Dad went over to Ireland for the funeral. On his way home he was sitting having a Guinness at Dublin airport having just said goodbye to his brother Dick who was flying home to London. While he was waiting for his plane back to Liverpool a light plane came crashing through the window of the departure lounge. With the luck of the Irish no one was hurt, not even the pilot, but it put dad off flying for a good many years.

That reminds me of a joke.

First pilot, "Jaysus, that runway was awful short."

Second pilot, "Yeah, but did you see how wide it was."

Dad never laughed at Irish jokes, I think he thought they were racist.

We went over to Ireland on the night ferry from Liverpool to Dublin. It was late when the taxi arrived to take us to the docks. We were all dressed and ready to go but had fallen asleep on the couch. We were very excited to go on a ferry for the first time, that was until we got out into the middle of the Irish Sea, it was a rough crossing.

We slept in a long narrow cabin with bunk beds along both sides, three high. We didn't get much sleep with everyone, including us, throwing up all night. The floor of the cabin was awash with vomit.

The ferry arrived in Dublin early the next morning and we were so happy to get off. We hired a taxi and set off for dad's ancestral home about an hour's drive away.

I should have been impressed with the beautiful countryside, but I was a city kid and I was already homesick. Actually, I wasn't just homesick, I was still physically sick. The taxi driver wasn't too happy when I wound down the window and threw up all over the side of his car. Dad's big home-coming had to be delayed until he'd cleaned the taxi.

It was 1966 and the radio in the taxi played the beach boys latest song, Sloop John B. The chorus of the song, 'I feel so broke up I wanna go home' rang in our ears.

For the next three weeks Catherine and I would sing that song every time a parent came into view. They must have been so disappointed with us, it can't have been easy saving the money to take us all to Ireland.

We were greeted by my Granddad and dad's sister, my Aunty Josie. I think they hated us on sight, and the feeling became mutual as the weeks wore on, and on, and on. Granddad looked ancient to me, but he was only in his mid-sixties. He was a tall thin man, slightly stooped with white hair. He wore his shirts with the sleeves rolled up and no collar. His baggy tweed trousers had turn-ups at the bottom, and he wore braces to hold them up.

Aunty Josie was a little woman, not much taller than me. She was also slightly stooped and a bit lopsided. She was crippled by rickets as a child from being undernourished as a baby. She was very bitter about that. She could get around well enough with two sticks, but she fell over a lot. Woe-be-tide anyone nearby when that happened, she'd lash out with her sticks yelling, "Jaysus, Mary and Joseph you pushed me over you feckin whores."

Rosaleen told me that on one of her trips to Ireland as a child Aunty Josie had come hobbling down the stairs carrying her full potty.

She'd lost her balance and tipped the entire contents over her head. I'd like to have seen that.

The family home was a cute little two-story whitewashed cottage. It had a porch over the front door with a black and white diamond pattern painted around it. There were sash windows on either side of the front door, and dormer windows at either end of the house under the eaves. There was a small garden with a picket fence, a gate at the front, and a vegetable garden to the side. There were rain barrels at the corners of the house to catch the water off the roof. I didn't appreciate the significance of this until later. No plumbing!

The two small bedrooms upstairs had sloping ceilings and windows looking out onto the fields. At the bottom of the narrow staircase there was a door leading to the scullery at the back of the house and another into the kitchen which was the main living area.

The kitchen had an inglenook fireplace with a black range which burned peat and cooked Granddad's daily breakfast, a plate of fried onions. A big wooden table stood in the middle of the flagstone floor with two bench seats and a chair at either end. There was a brand new kitchen sink unit under the window and a new electric stove standing beside it. They looked strangely out of place in that old farmhouse kitchen. On the other side of the kitchen was a door leading into a small hallway. The front door was to the left, and the door to the parlour was straight ahead.

I looked around and the first thing I noticed, there was no telly. Then I turned on the tap to get a drink of water, nothing came out. There was a white enamel bucket under the sink full of water. I was soon to discover filling it up would be our job for the next three weeks. Catherine and I would have to walk a mile down the road to the pump every day to fill it up with fresh water. It took two of us to carry it back. We'd come home soaked through, with the bucket half empty, only to be berated by Aunty Josie. "Jesus, Mary, and Joseph are you feckin useless altogether." She'd say.

We thought the up-side of having no water in the house would be no weekly bath. Every cloud! But dad threatened to take us down the road to the pump and hose us down in full view of the locals. But our ever resourceful mum found a tin bath hanging on the wall in the shed. So we had our bath in the kitchen in front of the fire, and the whole family. Could it get any worse? Yes, as it turns out, there was no toilet.

Dad said not to worry and went straight out and bought a camping toilet. It was just a bucket with a seat and visions of grandeur. Where should we put it? In the outhouse with the chickens at the back of the house of course, where else!

Let me tell you there is nothing worse than sitting on the toilet with a load of chickens peering at you with their beady red eyes. Dad had to empty the toilet down the bottom of the field every morning. He said he had to run fast because the flies would try to take it off him.

"Oh God! I feel so broke up I wanna go home."

On our first night in Ireland I was bored with no telly to watch so I wandered outside. I saw my Granddad sitting on an old wooden bench in the yard so I went and sat next to him and plucked up the courage to speak. "What do you do at night with no telly, Granddad?" I said. "I just gaze up at the stars," he said. I had a look and yes, it was pretty, but it couldn't compare with 'Batman,' or 'I Love Lucy.' I sat with him for a while because he didn't seem to mind me being there. I wish I had a photograph of that little girl sitting on an old wooden bench with her Granddad in his shabby old clothes gazing up at the stars.

There was no room for John and Kevin in the house so they had to sleep in the hay barn in the field at the back of the house. Not a good idea for John with his chronic hay fever, and Kevin with his asthma.

Kevin's lasting memory of Ireland is climbing in the window one night to get a glass of water and Granddad beating the living daylights out of him thinking he was a burglar.

Catherine and I slept in the parlour downstairs with Granddad. He'd given up his room for mum, dad, and Jayne. He slept in a single bed and we shared a double bed settee. Because the so-called toilet was outside there was a chamber pot under the bed for all three of us to use. I got out of bed to use it one night not realising Granddad had already filled it up. As I sat down on the potty it overflowed and came right up to my waist. I was soaked through.

"I feel so broke up I wanna go home."

One night I woke up to find Grandad standing beside my bed with his nightshirt hitched up around his waist. He was using the potty. I had no idea what I was seeing, but I felt a bit kinder towards Granddad after that, the poor man was obviously deformed.

I asked dad once what Granddad had done for a living. He told me proudly he was a road sweeper, and occasional grave digger for the council. I tried not to show my disappointment, I was hoping for something a bit more illustrious than that I have to admit. He then told me his father was one of the few people during the depression to have a job and there was always food on the table. When there are six hungry children to feed I guess that's all that matters.

Apart from saying she was a good cook Dad only ever told me one story about his mother. It was a story which shocked me to the core, and made me glad I never had to meet her, she died when I was three.

Dad said she was a little woman, only four foot nothing but she was fierce. She would have had very little in the way of possessions but her pride and joy were two porcelain dogs she kept on top of the dresser in her bedroom out of harm's way.

One day while she was out at the funeral of one of her parents, dad and his brother decided, for some reason known only to boys looking for mischief, that they would swing on the dresser. One either side rocking back and forth, it was great fun until both dogs fell off the dresser and smashed to smithereens.

Dad's mother came home and there was nowhere to hide. When she found out what they'd done she went crazy. She dragged dad out into the yard and put him on the chopping block, then picked up the axe. Luckily someone was there to save him before she chopped his head off. I'd like to think it was just a case of temporary insanity brought on by grief, but I do worry about the gene pool.

Granddad was a grouchy 'aul git.' He liked to sleep late in the mornings and didn't appreciate us kids playing in the yard outside his bedroom. He'd throw open his window and chase us. "Get out of it ye Fecking hooligans!" he'd say. I quickly learned to keep out of his way, but Aunty Josie was harder to avoid. She seemed to think we were just there for her convenience and should be put to work.

Aunty Josie had a strong Irish accent, I couldn't understand a word she said. One day she grabbed me by the arm and started ranting at me with her gibberish. She was pointing to two shillings she'd left on top of the stove. I had no idea what she was saying, but thought it was something about her going out and warning me not to steal it. As if I would, my thieving days hadn't started yet.

Not long after she'd left a man came to the door. He said he was the electric meter man and he'd come to collect his money. I told him everyone was out and I didn't have any money to give him so he went away extremely annoyed vowing to come back the next day, "And the money better be here," was his parting shot.

A short time later I spotted the two shillings on the stove and all of a sudden Aunty Josie's words fell into my brain the right way round and made sense. My blood ran cold! She'd been telling me to give the two shillings to the electric meter man when he called.

When she came home and saw the money still there she went berserk. "You stupid feckin eejit," She said as she lunged at me, intent on killing me stone dead. Luckily my mum was home by then, she pulled me behind her skirt and wouldn't let Aunty Josie kill me. I was right to worry about the gene pool!

Actually, I feel I should put in a kind word for Aunty Josie because she was nice to me once while we were there. I was sent down the road to the aul biddy with the cow every day to get the milk. The first time I went I wasn't sure what to expect. Did an 'owl biddy' mean she was a bird-woman? I was soon to learn everyone in Ireland was called the 'aul woman,' the 'aul one,' the 'aul fella,' the 'aul bastard,' or the 'aul git.'

One particular day I was sent down the road to get some milk from the 'aul biddy.' I started to feel faint. I could see a combine harvester coming towards me and knew I should cross the road incase he couldn't see me, but I couldn't seem to get my legs to work, that was the last thing I remember.

I came too as dad was carrying me back to the house. Aunty Josie looked genuinely concerned. "Take her up to my room and put her in my bed, its quiet up there." She said.

I'd never been in her room before and I was pleasantly surprised, it was such a pretty room. It was all ruffles and florals, very feminine with lots of nik-naks and jewellery on the dressing table. I couldn't relate the room to the woman I knew as Aunty Josie. It made me sad being in her room, Aunty Josie was only in her thirties at the time, but life had already passed her by. She never married, or had any children, which was probably for the best, she didn't seem to like them very much.

There was talk at one time about a certain Peter Mooney who lived down the road. He had a pig with a ring through its nose which I'm sure made him a good catch, but it didn't come to anything.

Mum and Aunty Josie took us to church one Sunday morning. Mum only ever came to church with us on Christmas day, so it was a special occasion. It took us a long time to walk there, with Aunty Josie hobbling along, trying not to fall over. It was a lovely day and all the locals stopped to comment on how nice we looked dressed up in our Sunday best.

We got to the door of the church and found to our amazement that we had to pay to get in. It cost a penny each and you still had to have money for the collection plate when it came round. I felt sad for all the poor people with big families who wouldn't be able to afford to go to church, and would burn in hell for all eternity as a consequence.

I sat there listening to the mass, not understanding a word as it was all in Latin. When the congregation recited the prayers it sounded to me like a giant whisper. I was desperate to join in, so I said over and over, "Whisper, whisper, whisper, whisper, whisper, whisper."

All of a sudden there was an almighty scream, and a woman sitting across the aisle threw herself on the floor and started writhing about.

We jumped up to gawp as kids do, but mum told us to sit down and face the front. The woman was carried out, she was obviously possessed by the devil. As soon as everyone got up for communion mum rushed us out the door. We didn't go to church in Ireland again.

There were a few serious accidents while we were in Ireland. One day dad decided to chop one of the plane trees down in the front yard. He climbed up and sat on the first branch about ten feet off the ground. He was happily saw-ing away not realising he was cutting the branch he was sitting on. And he wondered why people made jokes about the Irish. Down he went onto the road, he was lucky not to have been badly injured. I can still see him sitting in the kitchen with his legs sprawled out saying, "Oh God Jesus, the pain!" Just before I turned around and tripped over his legs. That was one time I was able to move faster than him.

Early one evening I was chasing Catherine around the yard when I tripped and fell, smashing my head open on the flagstones. She didn't see me fall and carried on running into the house. As I lay there going in and out of consciousness, wondering if anyone was going to come and help me, I saw a certain Peter Mooney looming over me. He was there helping dad cut down the trees. I was glad he'd come to rescue me until I heard him say, "Fecking kids, more trouble than they're worth." I could have warned my Aunty Josie she was wasting her time on him if she wanted a family.

Dad came out and carried me into the house, blood pouring from my head. I could tell from everyone's faces it was bad. We didn't have a car, and there was no phone in the house, but there was Granddad's old black bike. They could have put me in the tray and taken me to the doctor in town.

Aunty Josie was annoyed because they were all ready to go to the pub. Dad looked worried, but he was also desperate to get to the pub, and started hopping impatiently from one foot to the other. Mum told them all to go without her and she'd stay behind and look after me. So they did! How could dad do that when he could see I was seriously injured? Was 'the drink' really more important than me?

Mum wrapped my head in a tea towel, but the blood kept soaking through. I could sense her panic, she didn't know what to do next. Then she remembered the little jar of white crystals she'd gotten from our next-door neighbour back in Liverpool. He'd been an ambulance driver during the war and had kept a lot of medical supplies he'd used in the field.

Mum called it penacillin, but it was actually a clotting agent, it soaked up the blood and went hard, sealing the wound. A lifesaver for a wounded soldier, giving them time to get to a hospital for treatment.

No such luxury for me!

Mum wasn't sure if she'd remembered to bring the penicillin, she sent Catherine upstairs to have a look in the suitcase. I'm sure there would have been a few silent prayers said while she waited now that she was a fully fledged Catholic. Catherine came downstairs triumphant with the jar in her hand, I could feel mum's relief. She poured the crystals onto my wound but the blood-soaked straight through. She put another layer on, and it soaked through again. She kept pouring layer after layer until the jar was nearly empty. Finally the bleeding stopped.

She has told me since that she didn't know what she was going to do next if it hadn't worked, and she was never so glad to get home, back to civilisation so she could take me to a doctor.

I had a great story to write about when I got back to school, complete with a stick figure of me lying in a pool of blood. I remember getting a gold star for my efforts.

One of the beady-eyed chickens got some kind of disease and was looking a bit mangy, not surprising considering where it was living. Dad decided to put an end to its suffering.

We sat there laughing, watching him chase it around the yard trying to catch it. It's strange remembering him ever being young enough, or fit enough to do that.

He finally got the squawking, traumatised chicken cornered, grabbed it by the legs and took it over to the chopping block to remove its head. I presume it was the same chopping block where he'd nearly lost his own head all those years before. He should have been more sympathetic.

The axe was missing, so dad told me to go inside and get the bread knife. I watched in horror as dad sawed and hacked, trying to cut the chicken's head off. He hadn't even killed it first, so it was still squawking and flapping. Eventually, the head came off and dad let the chicken go. To my absolute amazement, it took off and ran halfway across the yard with no head before finally falling down dead. It added a whole new meaning for me to the phrase, 'running around like a headless chicken.'

That little incident was disturbing in itself, but the fact that the chicken turned up on our dinner table a few days later was beyond belief. Dad said he'd killed it because it was diseased, and yet we were expected to eat it. We refused of course, and had to put up with another torrent of abuse from Aunty Josie. Ungrateful fecking articles! Starving kids in Africa, etc, etc. I never could understand how my eating my dinner could stop some poor African kid from starving.

Toilets, or should I say the lack of, is one of my lasting memory of Ireland. The toilet had been invented, I know that for a fact because we had one in our house in Liverpool. And it was inside and upstairs, and it flushed. This particular luxury hadn't reached Ireland in 1966, well not the part my dad came from anyway. It may seem like I have a fixation with toilets, but believe me, when you've been without one for weeks it becomes something of an obsession.

I made friends with a little girl from down the road, she'd come over every morning and off we'd go exploring. There was plenty to see, and we spent many happy hours playing in the grounds of Trim Castle which was just down the road. It was over nine hundred years old. It's amazing to think of all the children in my family over the generations who would have played there.

There was an echo gate, and we'd have competitions to see how many times we could get our "Hellooo" to come back to us. There were also the ruins of an abbey with bodies buried in the walls. We scared ourselves senseless imagining we could see the bones of the dead people through the cracks.

My friend arrived one morning at the usual time, she was very excited. "You have to come to my house I've got something to show you." She said. So off we went for the short walk down the lane to her house. Her mum was very pleased to see me which I found a bit strange, no-one had told me we were related.

No doubt we were related to everyone within a two-mile radius, which would add weight to my concerns about the gene pool. All the locals treated us like royalty, dad was the prodigal son returned from the big city.

We went out into the yard and my friend pointed to an old shed, "Open it," she said. I lifted the latch on the rickety old door hoping she wasn't playing a joke on me and something horrible was going to jump out. The door swung open. "Holy Mother of God!" I exclaimed. It's amazing how fast you pick up the lingo. I couldn't believe my eyes, inside was a brand new toilet. The sun streamed in from the open doorway and glistened onto its pristine whiteness. I stood there for a few minutes paying homage to its beauty, then I stepped inside."What yer doin!" my friend shrieked. "Going to the toilet" I said. "No, no you can't. No-one's allowed to use it until my big sister comes home from Manchester, it was bought specially for her." "But no-one will know," I pleaded. "When's she coming home anyway?" I said, hoping to God she would say today. "Next month," she said. Irish people were strange I decided.

'I feel so broke up I wanna go home.'

We played in the haystacks in the field at the back of the house. We watched baby birds hatch out of their blue speckled eggs in the hay barn and we caught frogs in the stream.

Every morning we collected eggs with bright yellow yolks from the beady-eyed chickens. We ate fresh soda bread made with sour milk, and ate new potatoes dug out of the garden and boiled in their skins. Dad would peel them like an apple trying not to burn his fingers. He called them 'spudiaters.'

I wore my reversible shorts for the whole three week holiday. When the red and white stripes disappeared under a weeks' worth of dirt I'd turn them inside out to reveal nice clean orange and white stripes underneath and get another weeks wear out of them. They don't make clothes like that anymore.

So if nothing else the trip to Ireland was both eventful and educational. I think we left Ireland with considerably thicker skin than when we'd arrived. And even though I'd walked around with 'a face like a slapped arse' most of the time, it was a great experience for a city kid. It's one of my most vivid memories and left a lasting impression.

Dad's old house is still there. Aunty Josie left it to the Catholic Mission when she died and it's been sold a few times since then. It's been added onto over the years and is now unrecognisable. The yard where I sat with my Granddad gazing up at the stars is now a petrol station, the quiet country lanes are full of houses. I'm glad I got to see it the way it was when my dad was a boy.

12. CAMPING

We never went to Ireland again, we were introduced to a new phenomenon, the camping holiday. The older kids had all left home by this time so there were just the three of us younger ones left to enjoy the trials and tribulations of life under canvas.

It was a big tent, with a living area and two bedroom compartments, but there was no getting away from the fact that it was still just a tent. And apart from anything else, there were still issues with the toilet situation. We didn't even have a camping toilet this time, it was just a plastic bucket with a toilet seat on top. Catherine wasn't impressed with having to sleep in the living area, there was only room for me and Jayne in one bedroom, mum and dad in the other.

The day of our holiday would arrive and mum would be up at the crack of dawn loading up the car, and I mean loading! It was a little Ford escort with a roof rack. It would be so laden down with household paraphernalia the chassis would be almost touching the floor. We would be sitting on so many blankets, pillows, and sleeping bags, our heads would be rammed up against the roof of the car. We looked like the Beverley Hillbillies.

With two adults and a border collie in the front, and three kids in the back, the nightmare was complete.

The car was so heavy that on one trip to Wales we got halfway up a very steep hill when we started rolling back down. We rolled all the way down to the bottom and had to get out, taking as much luggage as we could carry out of the car. Dad drove the car back up to the top of the hill, and we all came trundling up behind.

We would set off, all wearing our matching hand-knitted Aran wool cardigans, or 'ganseys' as dad called them. They had real leather buttons in the shape of footballs. The only one who didn't have to wear one was 'Patch,' the Border collie.

Before we'd get more than a mile down the road, one of us would be throwing up and the dog would be throwing up all over mum's feet. Dad would never stop the car and let us out, so we had to use the makeshift toilet. Things got a bit messy when we all needed to use it at the same time, dad wouldn't even stop to let us empty it so we would have to put it on the floor between our feet and try our best to stop it from spilling.

So add to that smell, the smell of dog, the smell of a brand new car, and the cigarette smoke constantly swirling around our heads, not to mention the fact the windows were never opened, and it's no wonder we were all sick.

Dad wouldn't stop for us but he would stop at every pub along the way, and once the locals found out Mum played the piano we couldn't get away. She had a song list she kept in her bag, she could reel off one tune after another, and a great old sing-song would be had by all. Us kids would be left outside in the car park for hours with a bottle of lemonade and packet of crisps. By the time we finally got on our way it would be dark, dad would be drunk, and the arguing would start. We always got lost.

When we eventually arrived at a camping ground, if we were lucky enough to be staying at a camping ground, Patch would take off to find the nearest field and start rounding up the sheep. It must have been programmed into his DNA because even though he was a city dog he seemed to know what to do. One farmer threatened to shoot him, another offered to buy him. We couldn't part with him though, he was the best dog.

John had found him floating on a piece of wood in the middle of a duck pond when he was a puppy. He said someone must have tried to drown him. It was a good story, so he was allowed to keep him. Personally, I find it hard to believe anyone would want to drown a purebred Border collie, and with John's penchant for light fingeredness, I have my suspicions.

It was usually late by the time we arrived at our destination, and after getting lost numerous times the arguing would have reached fever pitch.

It didn't matter that we were all sick, tired, and hungry, we still had to put the tent up. It was the Rubik's Cube of tents, you needed to be a mathematical genius to put it together. All the poles were connected with wire inside so it should have been easy, but that didn't help us. We would cause such a disturbance with our fighting and arguing that sometimes the other campers would come and help us put the tent up just to shut us up.

Once we were unpacked dad would hook up the light to his car battery and things would settle down. It was quite cosy in the tent then, and didn't seem so bad after all. That is until dad unhooked the light from his car battery and left us in the dark with a torch while he and mum went to the pub for the evening.

It was scary, we had no idea where we were, or where they'd gone. We were used to being left on our own but not with just a thin piece of canvas protecting us from the outside world. We'd sit huddled around the table with just the torch and a transistor radio for company, watching the giant shadows on the walls of the tent as people walked past.

It's funny the odd things you remember from your childhood that have a profound effect on you. On one of our many nights alone in the tent, I remember listening to the life story of Bing Crosby on our little transistor radio. Dad liked him so I liked him too, we'd seen all his movies and loved his voice.

I'd thought he was such a gentleman so I was horrified to learn he was a wife-beater, and that his kids were terrified of him. I finally understood what the term, 'street angel, house devil' meant. He had this wonderful public image and he sang like an angel, but he was a 'house devil' just like my dad. I didn't like him for years after that. I did eventually get over my disappointment in him and he was allowed to sing at dad's funeral, after all, no-one can sing 'Danny Boy' like Bing.

There are three camping trips that stand out in my mind. The first one was to Snowden in Wales. It rained non-stop for two weeks, we were living in a quagmire of mud, our clothes and bedding were damp and cold. We had to be careful not to touch the sides of the tent or the rain would come through like a waterfall. After two weeks of misery most of the other happy campers had given up and gone home. Finally, the sun came out, and mum said we were going into town.

It was a Sunday, I know that because I was worried we would have to go to church. We were strictly non-denominational when we went on holiday, no mass on Sundays, and no confession on Saturdays. I thought it was a good compromise for having to endure three weeks living in a field.

I was hoping we'd be allowed to go up Mt Snowden in the little red train, but mum said it was too expensive.

We were all dressed and ready to go into town but Catherine had disappeared so mum told me to go and find her. I knew exactly where she would be, but I didn't want to go and fetch her as I had my new sandals and white socks on and there was mud everywhere. I gingerly picked my way along the path trying to avoid the worst of it. I found Catherine outside the swimming pool looking through a hole in the fence. We'd spent a lot of time there watching the other kids enjoying themselves. It cost money, so we'd only been allowed in once.

"Come and have a look at this," she said when she saw me. "How did you get over there?" I asked. She was surrounded by a sea of mud, but her clothes and shoes were spotless. "It's okay," she said. "Just walk across the mud, it's not deep. Look, I haven't got any mud on me." I didn't really believe her, but as usual, I took the bait. I took one step towards her and sank up to my ankles, my new sandals and white socks disappeared under the thick brown mud. Catherine was hysterical as she pointed to the mud-free path beside her that she'd walked along. I dragged myself out of the mud and trudged back to the tent knowing I was in big trouble. I didn't think I would be allowed to go into town, and couldn't bear another day cooped up in the sodden wet tent.

Catherine came running up beside me, still laughing hysterically. When mum saw the state of me she lifted her hand. I closed my eyes waiting for the sting. I heard a slap but I didn't feel anything. I opened my eyes, mum had slapped Catherine instead of me, and she was saying, "There! Now you can laugh on the other side of your face." To this day I have no idea what that means.

The second memorable camping trip was to Cumberland. It was memorable for one reason only, we were camped next to a rubbish dump. There was a lovely beach just over the hill, but we had to walk past the dump to get to it. On a positive note, there was a toilet at the dump, so we weren't lacking in amenities.

Being by the dump did have its advantages. Trucks would come in the night and dump all kinds of interesting things. One night they brought tons of crayons and colouring books. We spent most days scavenging to see what we could find. No-one believes me when I tell them we went camping at a rubbish dump, but there was actually another family camping there too.

This trip gave me the perfect opportunity for revenge, it was payback time for all the wrongs Catherine had done to me over the years. All her 'brilliant ideas' I'd ended up paying dearly for, and all the tricks she'd played on me.

We decided to go for a walk one morning and do some exploring. Catherine said she wasn't quite ready so she'd catch me up. I walked along the top of a hill and found a path leading down to the bottom. I was walking back along the bottom of the hill just as Catherine appeared at the top. "How did you get down there?" she shouted to me. Well, it seems there was a devil sitting on my shoulder saying to me, "Don't tell her about the path." "Oh, I just climbed down from where you are," I found myself saying. "Are you sure?" Catherine said. "Yeah! It's quite safe." I replied. She took two steps down and fell flat on her back into a pile of undergrowth. I started laughing, 'got yer, at last,' I was thinking. Then she started screaming. "What's wrong?" I shouted. "Stinging nettles! Go get help!" She screamed. She was getting stung over and over every time she tried to move.

I ran as fast as I could back to the tent. I told dad where she was and what had happened, and I just kept on running, I didn't want to be around when he pulled her out.

Hours later I crept back to the tent to meet my fate. Catherine was lying flat out on her camp stretcher, whimpering. She was covered from head to foot in Calamine lotion. I waited for the threats, the promises to get me back if it was the last thing she ever did, but she said nothing. She didn't know about my evil deed, and thought it was a genuine accident. I wasn't about to tell her otherwise.

It wasn't fair, whenever I tried to be evil it always backfired on me. Not only did I cause grievous bodily harm, but I had no-one to play with for three days.

On our final camping trip before we left England, we went to a camping ground in Norfolk. It had good amenities and even the weather was good. We were enjoying our holiday, as much as anyone could enjoy camping.

Dad went off to the pub one day and came back with a black miniature poodle puppy. He said he'd met a lady in the pub bemoaning the fact that she'd bought the dog for her daughter, but that she'd left home without taking it with her. Dad told the lady he would be only too happy to take the dog off her hands. We were thrilled, 'Patch' the Border collie had been gone a few years by this time, so we were ready to fill the void. It was the cutest thing, just a bundle of black fluff. It was also valuable. It came from a long line of 'Crufts' winners, and had a pedigree 'as long as your arm.'

Dad went back to the pub the next day for his usual drink and the bartender said the dog lady was looking for him. He said she wanted the dog back because her daughter had come home and was upset she'd given it away. We were surprised to see dad back from the pub so soon. He was in a panic. "Pack up, we're leaving," he said. "That 'whoorin bitch' wants the dog back." We were packed up in record time and with military precision. It usually took us all day with lots, and lots of arguing.

Rosaleen was living in Norfolk at the time, so we went round to her place and put the tent up in her front garden. We settled down to finish our holiday and everything went well for a few days until dad read the local paper. There was a notice from the dog lady, "Could the man from Liverpool please return my dog." Once again we packed up in record time and we went home. I was impressed, I thought dad had gotten so attached to the dog he couldn't bear to part with it. But I later found out he had big plans to breed from her and make his fortune. Unfortunately, she only ever had two pups.

One thing I did appreciate about the camping holidays was how much dad enjoyed them, he seemed so relaxed and happy and there wasn't so much fighting. After the initial debacle of getting there, and getting used to being in each other's company, we'd all settle down and it was fun, well sometimes. It gave us a chance to be a family without all the stresses of life and 'the drink,' getting in the way. I even remember dad coming outside and playing ball with us one day, he'd never done that before. I was a bit dubious at first, I didn't want to let my guard down, it could all end in tears. But I could see he was genuinely enjoying himself so I decided to take the risk and make the most of it while it lasted, it might never happen again. I was right!

Thirty years later I found out mum still had the tent so I thought it would be a good idea to take my kids to the beach and stay in it. Mum and dad met us at the camping ground and out came the tent. I wasn't prepared for the way I felt when I saw it, it brought back so many memories. I could feel the tension rising once again when it was time to put it together. I started to get nervous, dad was hopping from one foot to another, that was a bad sign. We decided to send him away on an errand. He left happily, obviously thinking he could fit in a quick drink or two while he was gone.

We laid the tent out and started putting it together. It was so easy, we had it up in no time. I felt bad misjudging the tent for all those years, it wasn't the tent's fault we couldn't put it up without a fight it was ours.

Dad eventually came back and was pleased to see it was all done. That was until the camp attendant came over and told us we were taking up two spaces and we had to move it. I could see dad was about to have a meltdown so I quickly whipped out the guy ropes, told everyone to take a corner and take four paces to the left. Its good to stay calm under pressure.

It was amazing sleeping in the tent that first night. I slept in the same place I'd slept all those years ago when I was a kid. I put my watch in the pocket on the side where I'd put my stolen treasures. Well, I had to steal, I never had any money.

I almost got caught shoplifting while we were on holiday in Wales. I stole some rock candy in the shape of false teeth. The shopkeeper saw me and chased me down the street. That was my closest call, and it was enough to put the fear of God into me and end my burgeoning career as a thief.

It wasn't all my fault, thieving ran in the family, and after all, I couldn't go home without a stick of rock for my friends. Dad would only give us fifty pence pocket money a fortnight. By the time we'd bought the necessary feminine requirements and the odd Mars Bar, there was nothing left. We'd beg him to give us a sub from our pocket money when we ran out, but he never would. He said if he did that we'd have even less to live on the next time. He said we'd thank him for it when pocket money day came round again but we just thought he was a miserable old git. He was right of course, and we were always glad he hadn't given in. That was a valuable lesson he taught me which I never gave him credit for.

So there I was experiencing the tent again after thirty years. The smell was the same, and I got the same claustrophobic feeling being zipped up into the bedroom compartment. The tent was the closest thing I still had to a childhood home. I couldn't go and visit my old bedroom, or see my old swing in the back yard, there was just the tent.

I woke up early the next morning, the air was damp and cold. I put my coat on over my pyjamas, and went over to the kitchens to make a cup of tea. I came back and sat in the awning, the same one mum had made all those years before. As I sat there thinking back over the all the holidays we'd had in the tent, it suddenly dawned on me...

I still hate camping!

13. EMIGRATING

Mum and dad went camping in Ireland the year before we emigrated to New Zealand. It was a farewell trip and the last time dad was to see his homeland. They didn't offer to take us. We were glad and annoyed all at the same time.

Life was just beginning for me that year. I was thirteen, I loved going to school, even though I wasn't very good at it, and I had some great friends. We'd take turns going round to each other's houses every Thursday night to watch 'Top of the Pops' and have tea and toast. In the weekends we'd go into town on the bus to try makeup on in the big department stores, dreaming of the day when we'd be able to afford to buy some.

All in all the year was shaping up to be a memorable one. I'd had my first drink in a pub, crashed a car, and survived a potential bomb blast. I also got drunk for the first time on two bottles of cider, the likes of which has never crossed my lips since. I also went to my first party.

I was allowed a lot of freedom when I was young, no one ever asked me where I was going, or who I was going with. I presumed it was because no one cared, but more than likely they just thought I was the sensible one and wouldn't get into trouble. And I didn't, well not much anyway.

On the night of the party I met up with all my school friends and we set off for the trek across town. The party was a long way away and we had to change buses about five times. Luckily my friends had a good sense of direction, I couldn't find my way out of a paper bag. Still can't!

There were boys at the party, one for every girl. I hadn't even spoken to a boy for three years so I was very shy. I needn't have worried, the boys hadn't come to talk. It was a boring party, no singing or dancing, just lots of snogging in corners, nothing like boys to put a damper on a party. I wasn't sorry when it was time to go home.

We made the long journey back across town, dropping girls off along the way when we reached their stop. Eventually there were only two of us left, me and my best friend Susan. Yes, one of the chosen no 'Z' in her name.

A bus came into view and she said, "This is my bus, yours will be along in a minute." "What! You can't leave me here by myself," I said, feeling more than a little scared. "You'll be ok," she said. I begged her to stay with me and she eventually she gave in, we both got on the next bus that came along. I got off at my stop and waved goodbye, she still had another three stops to go.

I still had a way to go before I reached my house. It was midnight and I was scared, so I ran all the way home. Not easy in platform shoes. The house was in darkness when I arrived. I was disappointed, I expected someone to be waiting up for me, to make sure I got home safely.

The next day I rang Susan to talk about the party and make up stories about how fabulous it had been. "I'm not allowed to talk to you," she whispered, "I'm grounded." I had to wait until I got to school on Monday morning to find out what happened. Apparently the bus she'd caught with me only took her one more stop then finished for the night. She'd had to walk the rest of the way. When she finally arrived home she found the whole family was out searching the streets for her. "You're so lucky," I said, thinking of my homecoming with everyone fast asleep.

Unfortunately nothing changed over the years and when my seventeen year old self rang up late one night to tell them my car had broken down and I was stranded, dad hung up on me. I rang back and thankfully mum answered the phone. She told me to get the bus home. The AA rescued me and got me safely home. Their parting words were, "I think you need to get yourself some new parents."
Oh! If only it were that simple!

The signs of future change had all started when we received a phone call in the middle of the night. It was a woman saying Our Kevin was dying and someone should come quick! Mum made a mad dash to New Zealand but by the time she got there he was fully recovered, he'd just had a bad asthma attack. Unfortunately, her first words to him were, "Why aren't you dead lad."

When she tried to come home, she found she'd bought the wrong ticket and wasn't allowed to leave the country for six weeks. She had no choice but to settle into the New Zealand way of life for a while. She found somewhere to board and got herself a job. The time she spent there was enough to convince her it was the place to be.

Dad was left in charge. He was well behaved for a couple of days, but then he started coming home more and more drunk each night. One night he came home completely legless and fell asleep in the chair. Catherine decided we should get him upstairs to bed so he wouldn't have a sore back in the morning. I told her he was too heavy for us but she thought we could manage. Another one of her 'brilliant' ideas!

She woke him up and we pulled him to his feet. We managed to get him down the hall to the bottom of the stairs. "Right!" She said. "Get behind him and push."

He was heavy, so it was slow going. About halfway up the stairs he started to lean back on us. He'd fallen asleep. "I can't hold him any longer," I said. "Neither can I," said Catherine. "Well that's just great, now what do we do?" "Okay, tell you what, I'll count to three, then run." She counted to three, we both let go of him and ran back down the stairs. We cowered under the stairs not wanting to see what happened next. He came crashing down, hitting the old radiogram at the foot of the stairs and ended up sprawled across the floor motionless. We waited for him to get up but he never moved. "Is he dead?" I said. "I think so," said Catherine. We didn't know to check for a pulse, or ring for an ambulance, we just stood there staring. "What should we do now then?" I asked Catherine, it had been her 'brilliant idea' after all. She thought about it for a minute then said, "We should go to bed, we've got school in the morning." So that's what we did. We stepped over him, and went upstairs to bed.

We got up the next morning and crept downstairs, not knowing what we would find. He wasn't there. We looked around and saw that his coat was gone so he must have gone to work. He wasn't dead after all. We saw relief and fear in each others eyes. Relief that he was still alive, and fear that he was still alive. I was worried all day at school wondering what would happen to us when he came home from work. I knew he would be angry with us for letting him fall down the stairs.

When he came home we made ourselves scarce and watched him from a distance. He just ate his tea quietly, then said he was going to bed because his shoulder was sore. He didn't remember a thing.

After that incident we decided we couldn't cope with him on our own so the cavalry was called in. Rosaleen arrived within a few days to whip us all into shape. Dad didn't know what hit him, he couldn't get one over on her. When he came home drunk we were told not to speak to him. I didn't like it, but it was the only way we could let him see his drinking was unacceptable. It wasn't a very effective way of dealing with the problem, if we'd stopped speaking to him every time he got drunk we would never have communicated, but we didn't have any other options. He hated being ignored. "So it's the 'no speaky' again is it," he'd say.

Mum finally arrived home with a big announcement, we were moving to New Zealand. We thought it sounded exciting and ran upstairs to pack only to be told we weren't leaving for another year.

I didn't understand what emigrating meant, I could only imagine it was going to be like a holiday, only not camping, that had to be a good thing. I had no concept of where New Zealand was, or that I would have to start a whole new life there

When Rosaleen heard the news she said, "You're not going without me." She packed up her family and moved in with us so she could save for the fare. The news wasn't so good for John. His wife understandably didn't want to leave her family, so he got left behind.

The day of our departure was drawing near, there was a lot to do. The house and all the furniture had to be sold. The garage door needed to be repaired after some teenage hooligan had driven through it a few months earlier pretending to be James Bond 007.

During this frenzy of activity dad decided he didn't want to go. He did his usual, and tried to drown his sorrows. He came home drunk every night, and there were terrible fights.

Slowly all our furniture started to disappear, every day when I came home from school there would be less and less in the house. What happened to our dressing table, the one that used to be Rosaleen's and now belonged to me and Catherine. Would the new owner's know why there was a line drawn down the middle of all the drawers? I realise now it would have been more sensible to have had a drawer each instead of dividing each one in half. All those years we spent pushing each other's clothes back over the line, so silly. It was almost as silly as having a window each, and a curtain each. If I was cold and closed my window Catherine would open hers, if Catherine wanted her curtain drawn for privacy I would open mine.

We even toyed with the idea of painting a line down the centre of the bedroom floor, but whoever was on the wrong side wouldn't have been able to get in or out without crossing enemy territory.

Where did the old oak wardrobe go with all our names scratched on the inside of the door showing how tall we'd been at different ages? And where was dad's favourite chair? I can still see him sitting beside the fire, smoking a rolled-up cigarette with his Sun Valley tobacco, strumming his fingers on the arm of the chair. I thought about all the years as kids we'd fought each other for prime position on the floor in front of his special chair.

I remembered Rosaleen as a teenager sitting in that chair while she got ready for a date. She'd be holding a cigarette, her hair in curlers, painting her fingernails while she listened to Doris Day on the record player singing 'Move Over Darlin.' She'd play it over and over with mum yelling from the kitchen, "Turn that thing off, you'll wear out the needle." The cigarette burns on the arm of the chair was a lasting legacy of those pre-date preenings.

Eventually, the house was empty. I was determined the new owners would know, 'Suzanne was here,' so I went around and wrote my name in every nook and cranny. Places that weren't easy to see and wouldn't be painted over and easily obliterated. After all you can't go through life without leaving a 'footprint,' or 'graffiti' in my case.

I went back to that house five years after I left it. I don't know what I expected to find. I think I'd convinced myself I could go back and my old life would still be there, frozen in time, just waiting for me to step back in. I would be able to forget about all the homesickness, the loneliness, and the longing to just 'go home' that had overwhelmed me so many times after we'd emigrated.

When I saw it again it looked exactly as we'd left it. The hideous orange plastic front door that we were so ashamed of was still there. I don't know what mum was thinking when she bought it, she probably got it with the Green Shield stamps collected from the garage. It was a Sixties psychedelic, bubble monstrosity. When anyone knocked on the door we could see them through the plastic running their fingers up and down in the grooves between the bubbles.

Looking at the house I could imagine Catherine hanging out of the top window risking life and limb for a challenge. I could see Jayne swinging on the front gate waiting to accost a passersby. I remembered the excitement seeing our John's car parked outside when I came home from school. It was sad, but without my family in it, it was just a house. I realised I'd taken the memories with me.

14. SAILING AWAY

We said goodbye to John in Liverpool the day before we sailed away to New Zealand. I don't remember any hugging or kissing, but then we weren't that sort of family. I couldn't help thinking, we're taking the dog with us, but we're leaving John behind.

We drove down to Southampton from Liverpool without stopping, except for a drink for dad of course. I was left to imagine all the things we might have seen along the way. "Could we stop at Blackpool and see the lights?" "No." "Could we call in and see Anne Hathaway's cottage?" "No." "Could we go to London and see Buckingham Palace?" "No."

We left England on 16th April 1974. Once we'd set sail we all went our separate ways and hardly saw each other except for meal times. Mum was seasick and spent most of her time in the cabin, and dad turned into Captain Pugwash.

Dad wasn't just impressed with life on the ocean waves, he was also impressed with the fact there were at least five bars open all day for him to choose from. So what with getting up at dawn, drinking all day, and breathing in the sea air, he was in bed straight after tea every night.

We were all in the same cabin except for Catherine, she had to share with Rosaleen and her family. Once again there was no room for her with the rest of us. It was horrendous for me as a teenage girl having to sleep in the same cabin as my dad, but our bunk beds had curtains and were fairly private.

Our cabin was at the bottom of the boat. We were below sea level, just above the engines and the noise never stopped. Even though there was a porthole, there was just blackness outside. I kept expecting to see fish swimming by, but there was nothing.

It was so hot and stuffy in the cabin. After a few weeks my eyes wouldn't open in the mornings. They'd be glued shut and I'd have to grope my way blindly to the sink so I could bathe them with warm water and try and to get them open.

First things first there was a life-boat drill. I refused to take part. I knew if I even imagined the ship sinking, it would. A few weeks before we left England we'd all sat down to watch our usual Saturday matinee on the telly. Unfortunately it was 'The Titanic.' We tossed up whether we should watch it or not, but curiosity got the better of us. Wouldn't it be better knowing what we were in for if things went wrong? Apparently not! It scared the living daylight out of us. We didn't know if we would be sailing through iceberg infested waters on our way around the world.

The issue with the Titanic sinking was that there were not enough lifeboats so that was the first thing I checked. But not knowing how many passengers were on board meant I couldn't tell if there were enough, there certainly didn't seem to be many.

I needn't have worried about sinking, we only went through one bad storm. We got thrown about a bit but no-one was badly hurt. When the sea was particularly rough, my friends and I would run as fast as we could along the corridors. By the time we'd get halfway down we'd be running on air as the ship lunged forward down the waves. The landings were a bit treacherous, but it's amazing what you'll do for entertainment when you've been cooped up on a ship in the middle of the ocean for weeks on end.

Every morning at the same time the intercom would spring into life. The Captain would announce how many knots we were doing, and how far we'd traveled so far. If you guessed right you could win a prize. I stopped listening when it dawned on me that every day he was taking me further and further away from everything I'd ever known.

After two weeks onboard it was pocket money time. I went hunting for my dad. It was a big ship but he wasn't hard to find. There were only a few places he could be and they all sold alcohol. He was in a good mood this day and even looked pleased to see me, a rare sight indeed.

I thought I might try my luck and ask him to buy me a Russian doll from the shop, one of those one's you open up and there's more inside, I'd always wanted one. It was five pounds, very expensive, but I assured him it was good value for money, it would last forever. He'd be pleased to know it was indeed good value for money, and it did last forever. I still have it, it's the only thing he ever bought me.

It wasn't long before we all got cabin fever. We'd been at sea for weeks with no sign of life when a cargo ship sailed by. Everyone ran to the side of the ship yelling and waving frantically. Once the cargo ship sailed out of sight there was a real sense of desolation. It was like we were stranded in the middle of the ocean, and our last hope of rescue had just sailed past.

Land Ahoy! Did they actually say that? I'm not sure, but if they didn't they should have. We'd arrived at the Panama Canal. I'd like to say I was impressed and overawed, but it was the most boring day of the voyage so far. Hours and hours of gates opening and closing. I have read that thousands of people died building the Panama Canal. They probably died of boredom. I for one didn't appreciate their efforts, if they hadn't made it so easy for people to sail to the other side of the world we could have stayed home.

We weren't allowed below decks because the engines were shut down. The air conditioning wasn't on and the heat was unbearable. We were told we could get off the ship at our own peril.

We saw guards on the docks with guns so we decided to play it safe, and stay on board.

While we were in Panama, a handsome young man came on board. I was standing by the railings trying not to stare when he came over to me and introduced himself. He asked me how old I was. "Twenty-two," I said. That was my standard answer even though I was only fourteen. He said he was twenty-one so I was kicking myself thinking he might not like older women. After chatting for a while he asked me to meet him for a drink in the bar that evening. I don't know what I was thinking, but I said yes, and didn't tell anyone what I was up to.

I got all dressed up in my new clothes. Red and black platform shoes, black maxi skirt, white satin top that showed my blue and white polka dot bra underneath. Gorgeous! I smeared on some 'Abba blue' eye shadow but decided against the false eyelashes Catherine and I had bought from the chemist especially for the trip. We'd tried the eyelashes on our first night at sea. We went up on deck but it was blowing a gale and the wind took our eyelashes and pinned them to our eyebrows, we couldn't close our eyes.

I made my way to the bar. He was waiting for me. He asked me what I wanted to drink. I didn't know. I wracked my brains and came up with a sweet sherry, that's what all the ladies on Coronation Street drank.

I was so nervous, I couldn't take my eyes off the window, I was sure dad would walk past any minute and catch me. I could just imagine what he would do if he saw me. He might not have minded that I was in a bar drinking, or that I was with an older man, but the fact that he was black would have sent him into conniptions. I'm sure he would have locked me in the cabin for the rest of the voyage.

Eventually I came to my senses and saw that I was probably getting in over my head. I ran off like Cinderella before I turned into a pumpkin, or before he cottoned on to the fact I was only fourteen. I kept a low profile for a couple of days until we reached Tahiti, he'd told me he was getting off there.

It seems odd to me now that the man got on the ship for such a short trip. He spotted me straight away, and came over to talk to me, which also seems odd in hindsight. When I eventually heard about all the people who disappear off cruise ships every year, I felt very stupid and very lucky.

We landed in Tahiti, got dressed in our best clothes and tottered down the gangplank in our platform shoes. Sea-legs, sand, and platform shoes and are not a good mix. After wobbling about sweating in our tights for half an hour we made our way back to the ship and got changed.

I'd never seen anything like it. There were no sealed roads and no pavements. The town was just a row of shacks all leaning on each other to stay standing. I started to get worried. What if New Zealand was like this? And how would we cope if it was as hot as Tahiti? Apart from a half-day bus tour around the island, and getting chased by a machete-wielding native when we tried to pick up a coconut off the side of the road, Tahiti wasn't very exciting. Then it was back to the ship, back to the tedium of shipboard life. But there wasn't long to go now. We were nearly there.

Foreign Land

What lies ahead in this foreign land
Will it welcome us give us a helping hand

Are there friends out there we've yet to meet,
who will open their hearts when they smile and
greet

Can we settle and build a new life for us there,
leave our past behind without any care

If we look to the future with much expectation,
and rise to the challenge with no hesitation.

Will life hold more than we thought was in store,
a much better life than we had before

15. NEW ZEALAND

We sailed into the city of Auckland at midnight. The lights gave a welcoming glow in the night sky after weeks of nothing but blackness and stars. It was so nice to see land instead of empty sea stretched out in front of us.

We lined up along the railings to get our first look at our new home. There were proper buildings, what a relief. I felt sick with anticipation and trepidation. Even though I'd had enough of being on the ship, it had become my home, I felt safe there.

The first thing that caught my eye was a group of people standing on top of a building waving a big banner. It said, 'Go home you Pommie Bastards.' I didn't know who the 'Pommie Bastards' were but I was glad I wasn't one of them. They'd just traveled halfway around the world, they deserved a better reception than that. I was soon to find out we'd sailed in on a tide of anti-British sentiment that was to make life very difficult for us.

I scanned the crowds on the dock hoping to see a familiar face, my brother Kevin. We thought he would have come to meet us and arranged somewhere for us to stay, but he wasn't there, and we had no way of contacting him.

We could have stayed on the ship overnight, but after four weeks we were desperate to get off, or disembark, the correct term for us seafaring folk. The taxi driver saw us coming and knew he could take advantage. We asked him to find us a hotel for the night and he drove us around the city for an hour, everywhere was full. Ours wasn't the only ship that had arrived that night, 'The Australis' had delivered its cargo of two thousand 'Poms' a few hours earlier. Eventually he found us one room in a hotel on top of a disco that thumped away all night. We weren't sure how far he'd taken us, or where we were, until we looked out of the window the next morning and saw our ship sitting in the dock across the road. He'd driven us round in circles.

Mum found some temporary accommodation in a camping ground at the beach. My worst nightmare, but at least we didn't have to live in a tent. Home was a log cabin on stilts. Wooden floors, wooden ceilings, wooden walls, and wooden bunk beds. I couldn't believe they'd brought us halfway around the world to live in a treehouse.

A week later mum said she was going into the city to look for a job and to see if she could find Kevin. She had no idea where to start looking but she was just walking across the street and she saw Kevin walking towards her. She brought him back to where we were staying, walked in the door with him and said, "Guess who I found?"

I sat on the beach wall, and watched through tears as our ship sailed away, my 'Robinson Crusoe' moment. Now I knew what it felt like, being abandoned on an island with no hope of rescue. I cried myself to sleep that night, but not before I'd made a promise to myself. I was going home first chance I got. I worked out it would take me five years by the time I'd finished school, got a job, and saved enough money for the fare. Five years and one month later I was on a plane flying home.

I'm sure there are ways of coping and adjusting to a new life in a new country, but we didn't know what they were. I think we were all in shock once the realisation set in of the huge changes we were going to have to live with. There was no going back. To make it harder, there was very little communication with overseas in those days. Phone calls were expensive, and if you wanted to call home on Christmas Day you had to book weeks in advance.

Luckily our John got a job as a linesman with British Telecom when he left the RAF so he was able to phone often, for free. He was usually braving the elements up a telephone pole when he called. If he was whispering we knew he was in a cupboard somewhere.

We'd left the 'aul' country but the problems came with us and the fighting continued, magnified by homesickness, loneliness, and frustration. I found out the hard way what you need to do to cope.

These are the rules for an immigrant family: 1. Stick together and be there for each other when the going gets tough. 2. Be understanding when one of you is having a hard time coping. 3. Talk things through. We did none of those things of course. We all went our separate ways and suffered in silence. When I tried to say how miserable I was I was told I was an ungrateful bitch, other kids would give their back teeth for such an opportunity. I didn't see opportunity, I just saw loss. Loss of home, friends, family, and identity. Who are you if you don't belong, if you're different from everyone around you? You want to hang on to everything that makes you who you are, but you're expected to fit in, which means changing so you don't stand out. Being told every day the way you've spoken your whole life is no longer acceptable, is very hard.

I should have been used to that, I was always getting told to speak properly at home, my Liverpool accent was very strong. But if you bring a child up in a certain place how can you expect them not to speak like everyone around them? Dad would say to me, "Why don't you speak 'proper' English, your 'vocalabry' is terrible." My reply to that was, "When you learn to pronounce 'vocabulary' properly, I will learn to talk 'proper' English." "Ooh you've got a tongue like a lizard," he'd say.

Everything was different in New Zealand. Our one family activity, watching telly together was over. The TV was black and white with only one channel. The programme's finished at ten o'clock and didn't start again until three the following afternoon. It didn't matter, we'd seen them all anyway, they were at least a year out of date. Coronation Street was five years behind. Five years! It was inconceivable to me that I would be an adult before I could start watching it again.

It may seem trivial, but Coronation Street has been one of the few constants in my life. We were conceived in the same year so there is a special connection. When they celebrate their milestones I celebrate mine.

The worst thing for dad was that the pubs shut at six o'clock every evening and didn't re-open until the next day. They were also shut on Sundays. His lifelong routine was over. Every day for as long as I'd known him he'd come home from work, eat his tea on his lap while he watched the news, then go off to the pub. On the weekends he would go to the pub after lunch, come home in the afternoon, have a sleep in his chair, eat his tea and then go back to the pub in the evening. Dad never drank in the house unless we were having a party. He liked to go out and drink and talk to all his cronies at the bar, that was his social life, now what was he going to do?

He was going to have a few drinks on his way home from work every day, then come home and take his frustrations out on me. I know he was lonely and miserable, but so was I. It was the last thing I needed.

Homesickness is a form of grief, its like losing a loved one. If you could only see them once more, talk to them once more, see something familiar once more. It leaves an ache inside you that you don't know what to do with.

Being called a 'Pom' upset dad. "I'm not a Pom, I'm Irish," he'd say. I was glad he was getting the same treatment as me, maybe now he'd realise his mistake and we could go home.

He picked on me mercilessly every day. All the older kids except Catherine had left home, and it was my turn in the firing line. He'd come home from work and start his usual tirade. "Why haven't you done this, why haven't you done that, you 'lazy whorin bitch,' sittin on your backside all day while I'm out working." He only ever saw the things I hadn't done, never what I had done. Nothing was ever good enough. One day I wrote a list of all the housework I'd done, and as soon as he started in on me I threw it at him. That took him by surprise and he left me alone, but not for long. Finally, one day I'd had enough, I threw caution to the wind, otherwise known as a death wish, and I answered him back. Gave him some 'lip,' or 'backchat,' as he would say.

He looked like he was going to explode, his eyes were blazing red, I knew I was in trouble. He had a rolled-up newspaper in his hand and he hit me with full force across the side of my head. I saw stars. He'd always threatened to knock me into next week, now I knew what it felt like.

I was never strong enough to fight back so I would use my only weapon, the one dad hated the most. Silence! The 'No Speaky…'

Everyone seemed to be getting on with their lives except me. Mum and dad both found full-time jobs. Mum worked during the day for the first time so she was home every evening, we weren't used to that and neither was dad. It just gave them more time together to fight, and added another personality to the simmering cauldron of our feuding family.

Catherine refused to go back to school and found herself a full-time job. Jayne was enrolled at the local intermediate school. I wasn't allowed to go to school, I was told we would be moving once mum found a house to buy so there was no point. I didn't mind, no school, how bad could that be? Pretty bad as it turned out, I got very isolated. The only thing I had to look forward to every day was dad coming home and telling me I was a useless lazy whore, and no use to anyone.

One night after a particularly nasty fight, I stormed out of the house, doing my best to slam the door off its hinges.

I went around the corner and just stood there, I had nowhere else to go. Mum came out, grabbed me by the scruff of the neck and dragged me back to the house. She threw me into my room, and slammed the door. It was as I suspected, the whole world was against me. I found out years later that she'd been afraid I was going to run away. If only she'd told me that at the time.

I started staying in bed all day. I stopped washing, and changing my clothes. There didn't seem any point, I didn't go anywhere, or do anything. It was Catherine who eventually noticed. She must have had a quiet word in mum's ear because she came storming into my room one evening, dragged me out of bed, threw me into the bathroom, and told me not to come out until I was washed. The next day I was informed I was going to school.

For a Catholic girl who'd spent the last four years in a convent school, the new school was an eye-opener. It wasn't exactly Sodom and Gomorrah, but it wasn't far off. Not only were there three pregnant girls in my class, one was pregnant to a married man. It was a whole new world for me. In my old school just being caught with a cigarette got you expelled on the spot. I don't know if the nuns even had a protocol for girls who got pregnant, but maybe I was just naïve.

The nuns did try to teach us sex education. I believe that's one of those 'oxymorons.' They held a special evening for the girls and their mothers at the school.

No-one turned up. I'm sure it wouldn't have been half as informative as sitting at the back of the bus on the way homeroom school listening to what the other girls had to say on the subject.

Smoking was the norm for most of the kids at my new school, and not just cigarettes. I'd never heard of drugs but they were everywhere. Marijuana was smoked and sold at school. You could smell it wafting up to the playground from the field during breaks. Most of the kids had a plant growing on their window ledge at home.

Even though I didn't fit in at school, no-one could understand me, and I couldn't understand them, I did make some friends. One of them was a Maori girl, she was my bodyguard. It seemed everyone wanted a piece of me. I was pushed downstairs and had things thrown at me, but I was left alone when she was around. I learned quickly it was no good being different so I started smoking and drinking and swearing like the best of them.

I didn't like drinking, and smoking gave me asthma, but swearing came naturally and it was all in a good cause. But I wasn't much of a rebel, no point being rebellious if no one is going to notice.

Catherine and I would go up into her attic bedroom and smoke to our hearts content. One day mum came up the ladder and opened the hatch, billows of smoke came down on her head.

She said, "If you can afford to smoke my girl, I won't give you so much pocket money." That was an empty threat, she never gave me any pocket money.

When I was fifteen there was an altercation in the kitchen resulting in Catherine getting a back hander across the face from dad. She stormed off to her bedroom and even though I thought she'd brought it on herself, I stormed after her. He was still the enemy, I had to show solidarity.

We sat on her bed smoking, trying to devise new ways of killing him when mum knocked on the door and came in. I quickly passed my cigarette to Catherine. If mum wondered why she was smoking two cigarettes at the same time, she never said.

My old Liverpool school friends threw me a lifeline by keeping in touch, but it could take six weeks or longer for our letters to circumnavigate the globe. Reading their letters was bittersweet. They gave me something to look forward to, but reading about all the things I was missing out on was torture. They were going to parties and on school trips, they were sharing their lives, growing up together. I was miserable.

I would never dream of telling dad how I was feeling, but he could always read my mind. He caught me at my lowest ebb one day wondering if I was ever going to fit in and make friends. He said to me, "It's no wonder you've got no friends, who'd be friends with you?"

I did eventually start to settle down, slowly and reluctantly. I was an obnoxious teenager. I couldn't possibly allow myself to be happy or appreciate anything, that would be giving in and mean they had won and not destroyed my life as I liked them to think. But imagine walking along a sandy beach to school every morning instead of the grimy streets of Liverpool with a scarf around my face so I wouldn't breathe in the poisoned fog. Taking my shoes off and paddling in the surf, instead of trudging through ankle-deep snow in leaky boots, and not being cold all the time. There are some things you can't argue with, but they didn't need to know that. Little things like that started to seep into my consciousness, but I was good at hiding my feelings. I wouldn't give them the satisfaction of knowing there were some things about New Zealand I liked. They had to be punished. Forever!

Even thirty years later when they moved to Australia I just had to say, "You brought us to this God-forsaken country and now you're leaving us here."

I did eventually learn to appreciate and be grateful, but it was hard, even soul-destroying at times. The life of an immigrant is not an easy one, and my youth got lost somewhere in the transition. I left school at fifteen and entered an adult world.

Our family life, such as it was, changed forever. We grew apart, and we moved away, it was nineteen years before we were all together again and that was the last time.

I went back to Liverpool when I was nineteen expecting everything to be the same, and it was, the only thing different was me.

When I went to visit my cousins and stood at the window of their flat which was on the top story of a block of maisonette flats it was brought home to me that I'd come full circle. I was born in a place like this, and as I looked out onto an ocean of concrete with not a tree or a speck of green in sight I knew I could never live there again.

For years I'd just wanted to fit in somewhere and thought I'd finally feel the relief of being the same as everyone else, but it was too late. I was like Alice in Wonderland after she'd eaten the cake in the glass box and grown too big for the room she was in. I didn't fit into my old life anymore. I was forced to realise you can't ever go back. Every new experience you have in your life changes you, and you could never be happy settling for less than what you've come to value. It was time to accept that and move on.

The years rolled by incredibly quickly it seems now. The family expanded. There were lots of marriages, lots of divorces, and lots of children born with no knowledge of the 'aul country,' or the way we were brought up. No understanding of what made us who we were, with our queer ways and strange accents.

16. THE LOOK

A year before dad died it was decided he needed to go into a rest home. He'd become impossible to live with, even more so than usual. His health issues had escalated and he'd been in and out of hospital. He was almost blind and had become a full diabetic needing injections every day. Mum couldn't cope with him anymore, he was making her ill. They'd been living in Australia for three years by this time, close to where Rosaleen was living.

She rang me one afternoon very distressed. Mum and dad had been fighting, and once again she'd been called on to come and sort them out. She couldn't handle it on her own anymore so she asked me to come over and help her deal with the situation.

I flew over from New Zealand the next day. I've faced many difficult situations in my life, but putting my dad in a rest home would have to be one of the worst, and one that will haunt me till the day I die.

Dad was back in hospital when I arrived, he knew he was in trouble when he saw me walk in. He knew I didn't like flying so it must be serious to get me on a plane. But mum needed help so I had to get there somehow. It's amazing what adrenalin will do to quell your fears, not to mention valium.

I flew over that vast ocean in a haze of tranquility, totally unprepared for what I would have to face when I got there.

I didn't know what to say when I saw him, even small talk escaped me, so I was relieved when he asked me to lower the back of his bed, it gave me something to do. Unfortunately I hit the wrong lever and he went crashing down. "God Jesus, what ye doin to me," he said. It was hard not to laugh.

The doctor came in and was most insistent we take him home. "It's not safe for him to be here," he informed us.

When the doctor left we tried to explain to the nurse that he couldn't go home, mum didn't want him back. It was falling on deaf ears, she didn't understand what we were trying to tell her, she just wanted the hospital bed vacated as soon as possible. He was our problem as far as she was concerned. Nothing new there then!

Out of sheer desperation I said, "Look, mum can't have him back, she's a battered wife. She's frightened of him." There! I'd said it out loud, and to someone who could finally do something about it. And I'd said it right in front of Dad. I don't know if he heard me, he was a bit deaf, but I suspect he knew what was going on.

The nurse's whole demeanour changed, and she launched into action. A nice rest-home was found close to where dad was already living so he could still get to his local drinking hole. He went quietly, but not happily. There was an air of hopelessness about him. That once again he'd been overpowered and outnumbered by the women in his life and there was no use trying to fight it. He knew if he could just get to mum he would be able to get round her and she would take him home. But she was sick, and tired, and refused to see him. She also knew he would be able to get round her and she would end up taking him home, she didn't trust herself to see him. As it turned out she never saw him again. She never went to his funeral, and she's never visited his grave.

I honestly thought she would take him back after she'd had a rest and was feeling better. I thought he was only going into the rest-home for six weeks of respite care. But after fifty-nine years of marriage, something inside her had finally snapped.

Rosaleen left me at the rest home with dad while she went and picked up his medication. I wanted to be anywhere but in that room with him. I kept busy hanging his clothes in the wardrobe, putting name tags on his clothes, trying desperately not to cry. It was humiliating, like he was a little boy going to school camp. He sat looking at me with those eyes of his, the eyes of my childhood, terrifying eyes blazing. Eyes that used say, "By Jesus, if I get my hands on you."

If Dad said, 'By Jesus' at the start of a sentence, you knew you were in trouble. If he said it at the end of a sentence, "If I get my hands on you, by Jesus." It meant he was in a playful mood, and we could relax around him. Seeing him sitting there so old and frail, it was hard to imagine ever being scared of him. I just felt sorry for him.

I thought back to other times over the years when I'd felt sorry for him. Those were just brief moments in time when I was paying attention. The time of the 'No speaky,' was particularly hard. And I know it hurt him when very early on we stopped calling him 'Pop.' It seemed to us it was more of an affectionate term, and he just didn't deserve it anymore. We'd started to notice what was going on around us and we didn't like what we saw. So we started to call him 'Father.' It was 'Father' who came home drunk, and it was 'Father' who gave us the hidings.

It was also decided not to let him kiss us goodnight anymore. I was about seven at the time, and it had always been a ritual of ours. Every night we would run the gauntlet of trying to pass his chair on our way to bed. He would grab us and rub his raspy chin on our faces. We would squeal and squirm, then he would pick all three of us up and run up the stairs, or 'up the dancers' as he used to say. He would have one kid on his back, one under each arm, and he would throw us onto our beds. We loved it, and so did he.

I remember the look on his face the first night we dodged his grasp as we passed his chair. After a few times he stopped trying to catch us.

I also remember his face the day he carried Jayne home in his arms covered in blood after she'd been savaged by the neighbour's dog. He looked so worried as he laid her on the back seat of the car and drove off to the hospital. I remember thinking maybe he does care about us after all.

He looked lonely the day he peeped his head around the bedroom door to see what Catherine, mum and I were up to. As teenagers we'd spend hours in the bedroom making clothes. The sewing machine was in mum and dad's room, and we used the bed for spreading the material out and pinning it to the pattern. It was all good until he woke us all up in the middle of the night yelling, "God Jesus, there's pins in me bed." I went back to sleep with a secret smile on my face that night. We weren't allowed to use his bed anymore after that.

I can still hear the anguish in his voice when I phoned to tell him Rosaleen had cancer. No-one should ever have to deliver that kind of news to a parent, and I swore I would never make a phone call like that again. But unfortunately I did, and the next time it was about me. I rang them on my way back from the hospital after getting the news no-one wants to hear. Mum answered the phone and said,

"Oh God!" I could hear dad in the background saying, "What! What now?" Mum shouted across the house to him in a big loud voice,

"SUZANNE'S GOT CANCER!" It's not the sort of thing people usually shout out in a loud voice, they usually say it in a whisper as though saying it quietly somehow lessens the blow. "Oh God Jesus!" Dad said.

Dad was happy to dwell on his own death but the thought of getting cancer put the fear of God into him. When he was a child his grandfather had come to live with them. He had cancer of the mouth and dad said he would hear him screaming in agony. Dad convinced himself that would be his fate one day too. When it didn't eventuate, he just told people he had cancer anyway.

His emotions were written on his face for all to see, if only we paid attention!

Up The Dancers

Up the dancers, one two three

come on dad will you carry me

on your back, I'll hold on tight

tossed on the bed, I squeal with delight

Every night is just the same

how I love our special game

Up the dancers, up the stairs

sometimes three, sometimes in pairs

One under each arm, and one on your back

just like a packhorse with an old sack

You heave us up with all your might

what better way to say goodnight

The whole time I was in dad's room at the rest home he never spoke, he didn't need to, I knew he was blaming me. I wanted to comfort him, to say things that would make it easier for him, but the past was crowding in like it always did when I was with him.

I'd made a point of not talking to him unless I had to over the years. You just never knew when he would come out with something hurtful, so I found it best not to give him the opportunity.

It was hard to keep the resentment at bay when cruel words echoed in my head of the many things he'd said to me over the years. Like the time he said to my husband before we were married, "What do you want to marry her for? She's just a bastard." Dad never liked my husband, which in my eyes made him an excellent candidate for a life-long partner.

The nurse came into the room and saw dad sitting on the bed looking dejected and sad. "What's wrong Tony?" she asked in her best cheery nurse's voice. I thought that was a stupid question when he'd just lost everything, and knew he was never going home. "I miss me wife," he said. I quickly turned away, tears were too close. "Would you like an ice-cream then?" Was this woman for real? "That would be nice," Dad said. That showed me how much I knew about dealing with this sort of situation, but then I'd never been in this sort of situation before.

As he sat there on his bed I wondered if he was thinking about how he ended up there, how it all came to this. If he was thinking about his life now that he was nearly at the end of it. Would he do things differently if he had his time over? Did he have any regrets about leaving New Zealand, ending up in a strange country at a time when the familiar is so comforting?

Rosaleen picked me up from the rest-home and we left with heavy hearts promising to visit the next day, my final day in Australia. We drove home in silence, and in tears, both tortured with our own thoughts.

We arrived at the rest-home the following afternoon determined to be upbeat and positive for dad's sake. We were impressed with the activity going on about the place. It was Friday happy hour. A singer was coming in to entertain the residents and they were all getting a glass of wine or beer, there was a real party atmosphere. The nurses were all very friendly, and quite a few of them were male, which I knew dad would appreciate. I started to cheer up a bit, as far as rest-homes went it, was a nice place.

We went down to dad's room to see if we could get him to join in the festivities. He wasn't there. We looked at each other both thinking the same thing. He'd escaped! We notified the staff and started to search the rest-home. One of the nurses was sent to scour the neighbourhood. Dad's house was just around the corner so we were worried he might have tried to go home.

Mum was at the house and we didn't want him confronting her when she was on her own. We still felt it was our job to protect her from him even at this late stage in their lives.

We couldn't find him anywhere. All the bad memories from years gone by made the fear and panic rise up and nearly choke me. Then Rosaleen said, "Listen." "What is it?" I said. "That cough," She said, "I'd know it anywhere." We followed the sound and found dad sitting in a corner of the lounge, partially obscured by a big pot plant. He'd found a good vantage point to sit and watch the comings and goings of the other inmates. He could sit there without being disturbed while he got the measure of everyone, sort out the gobshites from the halfwits.

When we told him about the glass of beer he agreed to come and listen to the music, he'd do anything for a drink, but he refused to sit with the others. He wanted to keep himself apart, he wasn't rest-home material just yet.

When we were all settled in the lounge and dad had his hands wrapped around a nice cold beer, which we knew would keep him quiet for a while, Rosaleen looked over at him and said to me, "He's too young to be in here." He was eighty years old and half-blind, but I knew what she meant.

Dad had been allowed to take his canary to the rest-home. It was on the window-ledge in the communal lounge. When the music started the canary whistled and trilled and sang his little heart out, he drowned the singer out. The bird seemed particularly fond of Elvis songs. It was hilarious, everyone was laughing, except dad.

Canaries had been a part of dad's life ever since John brought one home from one of his trips to sea. He'd bought two but one died on the voyage home. John put it into a cigarette box and buried it at sea.

The canary's cage was kept on the window ledge in the living room of our house in Liverpool. Dad loved to whistle and make the bird sing.

Unfortunately John assumed mum would look after the bird, and mum assumed Kevin would look after it. So the canary died from a tragic case of cross purposes, and starved to death.

Many years later dad got another canary. This one was well looked after, in fact it was killed with kindness. Like any responsible pet owner dad had to clip the bird's toenails. Dad was concentrating so hard on the task at hand he didn't know he was holding the bird too tight. He did a great job with the toenails, but when he'd finished and said, "There you go Jimmy, all done," the Canary was dead.

Not to be deterred, he got another one, but he had to leave that one behind when he moved to Australia. A week after dad was buried, Jimmy Mark 2 went out in sympathy and fell off its perch stone dead. It seemed only fitting to bury it with dad, but he's not mentioned on the headstone.

So the Canary was a great success at the rest home and it helped break the ice for dad. The other residents started coming over to talk to him. He didn't answer them of course, but it was a start.

We were pleased to see the old Irishman there that dad had met while he was in the hospital. He'd had a fall and badly damaged his leg so he and his wife were moving into the rest-home together. It was a sad sight seeing them sitting there not knowing what was going to happen to them, and if they'd be allowed to stay together. They mentioned they had a son living in another city. He should have been there with them, they looked so scared. It was a sad ending to a long life together.

Dad wasn't interested in being friendly with the Irishman but it had given him the idea that mum could move into the rest-home with him. That showed how confused he was about the situation he was in. He didn't seem to have any concept about why he was there, and why he couldn't go home to mum and carry on as normal. They'd had their ups and downs in the past and she'd always come round, why should this time be any different?

He was like a child that was finally getting punished for something he'd gotten away with many times before. He didn't understand what he'd done wrong, so once again he looked around for someone else to blame. That would be me.

The singing was finally over and it was time to go, time for me to say goodbye. I was dreading leaving him there, I knew I might never see him again. He walked with us to the front door. He gave us both a hug and then he gave me a look I'll never forget. That look said: How could you do this to me? Don't leave me here. I'm your father. I hate you for this. Well, you can kiss me arse!

That was the last time I saw him.

The Look

The Last time I saw you, you gave me The Look

your face so transparent, it read like a book

Don't do this to me, don't leave me here

a face full of sadness, loneliness, and fear

It wasn't my doing, it wasn't my place

I didn't deserve that look on your face

17. THE PENSION

I had to cancel dad's pension after he died. It wasn't as bad as I thought it might be, just a few forms to fill out, names, dates, sign here, and it was done. Stepping out of the pension office onto the pavement a memory came flooding over me like a rain shower. I'd forgotten until that moment that I'd been with dad the day he applied for his pension.

He'd been was worried about having to fill in the forms because he couldn't write very well. Those nuns might have been handy with the whips, but they weren't very good teachers. He didn't see why he should have to go to the same place where people signed on for the dole, he was afraid someone might see him and think he was a bludger. I convinced him it wasn't a hand out, it was a pension. He'd worked all his life and paid taxes, he'd earned it. He didn't look convinced, so I offered to go with him and help him with the paperwork.

There was a hair-raising drive into town ending when he hit the wall outside the pension office, he was a terrible driver. He was forty before he got his driver's license. He'd had to sit the written test five times before he passed it. He was so nervous going for his driving test that mum put some whiskey in his coffee...

We went inside and were told to take a seat. Dad sat down trying his best not to be noticed, he looked so uncomfortable.

His name was finally called and he ran up to the counter, leaning right over. He answered all the questions in a whisper so no one could over-hear him. he hated anyone knowing his business.

Even good news had to be kept private in dad's eyes. I was ten years old when Rosaleen rang to say she'd just given birth to her first child. Dad said, "Now don't you be tellin the whole street, its none of their business." Everyone in the street knew Rosaleen and were waiting to hear the news. So as soon as dad left to go to the pub we went knocking on all the neighbours' doors spreading the good news. I was an Aunty, people had to be told.

I got my first job at fifteen and wore a uniform to work. Dad said, "You shouldn't be wearing that uniform on the bus, you don't want everyone knowing where you work." I don't know who 'everyone' was, but I was proud of my new job and didn't mind 'everyone' knowing.

When dad moved to Australia he complained no-one in the club would talk to him. I had a brilliant idea. I bought him a shirt for Christmas and had New Zealand embroidered in small letters over the pocket. I told him it would encourage people to talk to him as there are lots of Kiwis over there. He never wore it. "Don't want all them gobshites knowing my business," he said.

Dad liked to keep the world at bay, but he liked to know everyone else's business all the same.

Back at the pension office all the forms were filled out without any drama and dad had signed his name in all the appropriate places. It was a lot easier than he'd thought it would be, but still, he was glad it was over. He was ready for a well-earned drink. He always was.

And so there I was all those years later standing on the pavement when I realised there wouldn't be any more forms to fill in. He's not in the system anymore, he ceases to exist. It's so final. I hoped no one noticed the tears as I walked down the street.

Our lives are ruled by paperwork. Forms, certificates, pay-slips, a paper-trail tracking our lives from start to finish. A week after dad's funeral I got his death certificate in the mail. That was it, all the paperwork complete.

The Last form

I opened the letter and there you were
all that was left of you hiding in there

I drew it out slowly not wanting to see
what it would tell me, what would forever be

The last form filled out announcing your death
held in my hands while I held my breath

How could I read it but how could I not
there's nothing left now, it's all that I've got

18. SUMMING UP

So when did my relationship with my dad go wrong? How did a young girl who was once her dad's favourite end up with no relationship with him at all? Can I see now after writing all this?

It started out well for me, I thought I had the best dad in the world. All kids think that, its up to the dad to keep that feeling alive. It's not easy, but kids know when you're doing your best.

Dad was always telling me I should have more respect for him. I wanted to tell him you have to earn respect and that I deserved respect too. He thought he could get undying love and devotion from his children without earning it. I felt a real sense of disappointment in him when he saw that I wasn't prepared to love him no matter what.

His death left me looking for answers to questions never asked. It's amazing how long you can live with something festering inside you, and the very minute you lose the opportunity to explore it is the very minute you want to.

Brothers and sisters become important then, they were there, they know and they might have some of the answers. You talk and talk, and it does help, but it also makes you realise you're not the only one who was damaged, there were six of you and that's sad.

Six people who had to go out and start families of their own. How could we do that successfully with no decent role model? Could we break the cycle of abuse, or was it too ingrained in us? Did we have the alcoholic gene that runs through families, therefore giving us no choice?

Some might say ours was a dysfunctional family. I don't think so, I think we were just the children of a dysfunctional marriage. Jayne once described their marriage as 'a crime scene that's never been investigated.' Sometimes it seemed as though they didn't so much get married, as start a war.

Our family functioned as well as any other most of the time, we were well dressed and well-fed, well sort of. Cabbage and potatoes for dinner every night might not be considered well-fed, but we never went hungry. Our physical needs were taken care of, and we always had a home to go to. It wasn't the best family life, but it was mine and the only one I wanted. I can hear that song in my head right now,
'Always Look on the Bright Side of Life.'

There was definitely neglect on an emotional level, but it was a different time and people weren't as in tune with their feelings as they are today. The only real emotion we could get away with was anger, there was plenty of that in our house. We understood anger, we knew where it would lead. 'Its better the devil you know.'

We weren't allowed to cry. When we were small we would be told, "Quick, let me kiss it better." That gave me the message crying upsets other people. As we got older it was, "Stop crying, you big cry baby." So, it was humiliating if other people saw you crying. When we got older still, it was, "I'll give you something to cry about in a minute." The fear of showing emotion sets in. So we learned to suppress our tears and laugh instead. When you do that for long enough you become too afraid to cry. You feel if you start you might not be able to stop, and then what? You don't know it's impossible to cry forever and the worst that can happen is you end up looking like a pufferfish.

Tears wash away the barriers to your emotions enabling you to feel and move on. If you swallow the tears they get stuck in your throat forever. Unshed tears are a heavy burden to carry.

No one knows what lies ahead for them but 'as long as your arse is pointing to the ground,' as dad used to say, meaning as long as you're still standing, you're still alive, so you should try to do your best. The past still haunts, and it's a constant battle not to revert to old habits when things get tough.

I think the lesson I learned is don't have children unless you really want them, then take the Hippocratic Oath, 'First Do No Harm.'

I'm grateful to my dad in some ways. He showed me what I didn't want in a husband. All my boyfriends were given the same ultimatum. "You ever lay a finger on me and you'll never see me again." It probably wasn't a good opening line on a first date, but I didn't care, a girl's got to protect herself.

Dad showed me what I wouldn't tolerate in a marriage, and he showed me the type of father I didn't want for my children.

Someone once asked me what was my 'definition of success.' An image came to mind of my youngest son when he was about seven years old. He was sitting on the lounge floor playing a game when he heard the front door slam. He jumped up and said, "Dad's home!" I looked at him and saw no fear in his eyes. I knew then that was it, My 'definition of success.

Your childhood is what it is, its up to you not to let it ruin your life and your future relationships. It is difficult at first. When you're young you can be drawn to someone like your father, there's an instant recognition and you can get confused into thinking it is something else. You feel as though you've found your soul mate because they are so familiar when really they are just mirroring your past. And so the cycle can begin again.

What Lies Ahead

No-one knows what lies ahead
what life will have in store
For some of us the future tends
to mirror what's gone before

Be careful when you make a choice
to follow a well-worn trail
Is it right for you, will it bring you joy
allow happiness to prevail

Seeing mistakes that others made
can surely be a gift
If you learn from them and take a stand
cut the old ways adrift

You can make your future rich and full
by doing things your way
Suffering, pain, and hardship
a price you'll never have to pay

We brought dad back to New Zealand and gave him the best funeral anyone could wish for. He would have loved every minute of it. He didn't deserve it of course, but what can you do, the living have to do what's best for them. And after all, don't we have to prove to ourselves we're not like him, that we can put the past behind us and forgive?

But then again, were we still trying to get his love and approval even after he was dead? Would he know the lengths we'd gone to to give him a good send-off? Would he have appreciated it? I'd like to think so, but I couldn't say for sure.

A month after the funeral it was dad's birthday and once again we were looking for the perfect gift. We got him a beautiful green headstone in the shape of Erin's Harp with a shamrock engraved above the inscription. Even he would have approved of his final gift.

Epilogue

Many years ago I wrote a few children's stories based on my childhood with Catherine. I optimistically and naively sent them off to a publisher. A boomerang wouldn't have come back any quicker.

I went round to see mum and tell her about my rejection letter. Dad was in his usual prone position, feet up lying back in his recliner chair doing his daily thumb exercises on the remote control. I just ignored him as I usually did. He was never interested in having a conversation anyway unless he was the centre of it.

I started telling mum about my stories being sent back. "Well, you don't want to give up. Just because one publisher didn't want them someone else will, you have to keep trying." To my amazement it was my dad talking, I didn't even know he was listening. What's more, I didn't think he knew anything about anything other than the price of beer. He lived on the sideline of life, never wanting to participate in anything. He'd never given me any encouragement in my life, except for whistling, and telling jokes, but there he was encouraging me to write. I wonder if he would have been so supportive if he'd known what I would end up writing about.

Dad never read a book in his life. He wouldn't have read this one either.

Some memories you keep in your head, and some you keep in your heart.

The early years with my dad were my happy time, those are the memories I keep in my heart.

You Can Go Home

You can go home, be prepared to allow
memories to surface, refused until now
Buried down deep for so many years
hiding your anguish, your sorrow, your fears

You can go home, with an open heart
full of forgiveness, wisdom to impart
Understanding yourself, knowing who you are
there's peace in the knowledge, you've come so far

You can go home, face the ghosts of the past
they've no power to hurt, you're free at last
In charge of your mind, at peace with your soul
there's strength and courage, now you feel whole

You can go home, in your mind, in your head
the place long gone, the people now dead.
You've become who you are because you were there
learned life's lessons of happiness, not despair

ABOUT THE AUTHOR

Suzanne Butler lives in New Zealand with her
husband of thirty five years.
She has two grown up sons
This is her first novel

Printed in Great Britain
by Amazon

34109683R00127